ENDORSEMENT

As I read the manuscript for Mario Murillo's new book, *Vessels of Fire and Glory*, I said to myself, "Finally!" Mario has measured the Church and the nation in this season and did not hold anything back. His honesty is like the sun rising inside a dark cave. This release is a paradox—it is sobering and refreshing; it is symptoms and the cure. I believe this revivalist has penned a treatise that should be in the hands of all who lead the work of God.

JOHN KILPATRICK
Founder and Senior Pastor
Church of His Presence
Daphne, AL

VESSELS *of*
FIRE &
GLORY

VESSELS *of* FIRE & GLORY

BREAKING DEMONIC SPELLS OVER AMERICA
TO RELEASE A GREAT AWAKENING

MARIO MURILLO

DESTINY IMAGE® PUBLISHERS, INC.

P.O. Box 310, Shippensburg, PA 17257-0310

"Promoting Inspired Lives."

This book and all other Destiny Image and Destiny Image Fiction books are available at Christian bookstores and distributors worldwide.

Cover design by Eileen Rockwell

For more information on foreign distributors, call 717-532-3040.

Reach us on the Internet: www.destinyimage.com.

ISBN 13 TP: 978-0-7684-5161-0
ISBN 13 eBook: 978-0-7684-5162-7
ISBN 13 HC: 978-0-7684-5164-1
ISBN 13 LP: 978-0-7684-5163-4

For Worldwide Distribution, Printed in the U.S.A.
1 2 3 4 5 6 7 8 / 24 23 22 21 20

CONTENTS

FOREWORD

WHAT MAKES A SPEECH OR A PIECE OF WRITING great? If I said, "I have a dream," most informed Americans would recall the historic message from Martin Luther King Jr. during the civil rights movement. If I said, "The Emancipation Proclamation," immediately Abraham Lincoln would come to mind, along with one of the shortest speeches ever given (272 words), "The Gettysburg Address." Today the speakers who made these words famous are entombed in monuments of marble, but their words are still living, etched on buildings and printed in thousands of books. The cliché, "the pen is mightier than the sword," has been proven, especially when sinners are converted after hearing or reading the words of the prophets and apostles recorded in the Bible.

Vessels of Fire and Glory was penned under divine inspiration and spiritual revelation as the Holy Spirit spoke to Mario Murillo. He is a man who is a voice and not an echo. He is more of a prophet than a pulpiteer. His office is an evangelist, but his assignment is to warn America, especially the Church, and pull the showtime curtain down, exposing an anemic Christianity, a toothless "churchianity" so weak that it cannot take a bite out of sin and whose theme should be, "Come as you are and leave the same."

In an age when technology is more important than theology, and Sunday services leave Jesus outside knocking on the door trying to get into His Father's house, we are either on the edge of a

1

national revival or a riot. Without a true humbling and a break-through, this nation is at a tipping point of disaster.

However, in this book, which is more of a manifesto, the false is exposed, the truth is declared, and the fire of hope is handed to the reader. This book will ignite the reader's own personal God encounter that can set them on the course for the last end-time revival. Read these words and allow them to soak into your spirit and transform your thinking.

When Samson was at his worst moment in life, blind, bound, and going around and around, grinding at a millstone, he cried out for God to remember him "one more time." His prayer restored the anointing and brought the house down on his enemies. His last move of the Holy Spirit was his greatest. There is a generation marked for one last outpouring—the greatest. Will we cry out like Samson and be restored to the fullness of the glory of God? Let this book help lead you into your God assignment.

Perry Stone Jr.
Founder of VOE, ISOW and OCI
Host of *Manna-Fest*

SECTION I

Introduction

THE GODSEND

ID YOU EVER WONDER WHY GOD ISN'T DOING something? You see America being torn apart, battered into submission, and molded into some ugly weak version of her former self. All in the name of progress. When the moral bottom of society becomes the loudest voices of influence, shouldn't God act?

I believe He is acting. But it is happening in a wholly unexpected way. He is at war to save our nation. The real question is, are you ready to understand what your assignment is in His war to save America?

In a last-ditch effort to save America, God will pour out His Spirit. It will not be within the "system" but outside celebrated circles. It will restore much of the Spirit-filled Pentecostal churches from business-model entertainment centers back to a movement. Many small churches will become ground zero for the glory of God.

This event will not be painless. Wicked agendas will topple. False doctrine will die an early death due to the healthy appetite of young converts. Church empires will be given the ultimatum to return to dependency on the Holy Spirit or suffer total loss.

His miracle will be a great boon to some, but a horrendous event for others. It will be a day of rejoicing and mourning. A panoply of extremes.

If you think the next revival is something to grow your church—forget it! This time it will be an act of war. It must topple man-made religious empires led by those who are traitors to their original calling. It must raise up those unknown and unesteemed to places of power and influence.

Saving a nation in our condition can't be painless or comfortable. The kind of moral awakening God prescribes for us must be messy and glorious.

Take Acts chapter 5 as a model. The casual observer would be stunned and baffled. On the one hand, God is using the shadow of Peter to heal thousands in the streets. On the other hand, God is killing people in church. The day of the Lord is darkness and light, blessing and judgment, healing and death. The day of the Lord is one of the only things described in the Bible that evokes equal parts yearning and dread.

Take Amos 5:18 and Psalm 110:3 as examples:

> *Woe to you who desire the day of the Lord! For what good is the day of the Lord to you? It will be darkness, and not light.*
>
> *Your people shall be volunteers in the day of Your power; in the beauties of holiness, from the womb of the morning, You have the dew of Your youth.*

In the lead-up to this miracle, God is working on two sides of the street. On one side is the Lazarus generation and the other side is a prophetic core.

Out of graves in the inner city and on campus, the Lazarus generation will rise. Today they are in gangs, on drugs, or screaming for leftist revolution. Then, in a way no man can take credit for, they will be struck by the resurrection power of Christ. Tomorrow they will be baptized in the Holy Spirit and will operate in frightening zeal.

Meanwhile, the prophetic core wanders, feeling outside the mainstream. They have been ostracized for wanting revival. They have been punished for not getting with the slick programs. They have huddled together to pray and compare notes. They are starved for the fire, glory, and presence of God. They feel helpless and forgotten, but in their weakness they are being made strong.

At the moment of power, the day of God's power, these groups will collide. The core that yearns for revival doesn't know they are being forged to be the fathers, mothers, brothers, and sisters of resurrected youth. We will see a new fulfillment of Matthew 11:12, *"And from the days of John the Baptist until now the kingdom of heaven suffers violence, and the violent take it by force."*

The Lazarus generation will find church—as we know it today—unbearable. Only this radical core will understand from their own brokenness how to "loose them, and let them go."

You may remember the Jesus movement. You may recall that as older Christians were receiving the baptism and leaving mainstream denominations, hippies, addicts, and campus radicals were being saved.

Barefooted, long-haired youth invaded churches in Southern California. Some churches turned them away. Pastors like Chuck Smith and Ralph Wilkerson embraced them and saw explosive growth. Eventually, millions were saved nationwide.

The hallmark of that revival was acoustic, gentle choruses and a message of unconditional love. This reflected the gentle love matrix of the hippie movement.

Remember, Jesus is seen as both Lion and Lamb. The Jesus movement expressed His lamb nature...now comes the lion. The plaintive cry will now give way to the prophetic roar.

Out of the matrix of today's death metal, gangsta rap, violent protest, and intense division, young lions will emerge who will fulfill Joel 2:28, *"I will pour out My Spirit on all flesh. Your sons and your daughters shall prophesy."*

Whereas the Jesus movement was marked by the gift of tongues, we will now see tongues of fire and prophecy. The prophetic gift will be delivered from the fleshly parlor tricks in which it has been imprisoned to nation-altering status. It will prophesy truth to power with paralyzing conviction.

God is issuing fair warning. He is recruiting those who will abandon the corrupted forms that cling to many believers. He is sending out a call to submit to preparation.

Writing this book took more out of me than I ever imagined.

A. W. Tozer, who said he took no delight in preparing a certain message "because of the reality of meeting Satan's opposition head-on":

> I have never given more time and more pain and more prayer to any other series of sermons in my ministry. Because of their importance, I have literally felt Satan attempting to thwart the purpose of God. I have felt I was in raw contact with hell. There are so many in the Church who are spiritually blind that I tell God

that I want to be able to see—I want to be a lower-case "seer." I want to penetrate and understand and have discernment concerning the whole plan of God. I want to appraise the situation and see it as God sees it—to know the role of God in this day of religious confusion.[1]

I would never compare myself to Tozer, but his experience resonates deeply. When I was asked to write this book, my first thought was about how viciously the devil would attack me. When I began writing, the attack was worse than I imagined.

This message exposes a condition among believers that Satan fiercely tries to hide. But it must be exposed.

After fifty years of ministry, I have seen every doctrinal float in the parade. I have witnessed a new generation getting thrilled by the "newness" of something that had passed through the Church many times before.

One float has lingered way too long—the spiritual entitlement float. This is the idea that God is so taken with us He has overruled His character in order to humor us and pamper our consumerist Christianity.

Entitlement permeates our videos. It oozes from our conferences. It colors our definition of faith and grace. Entitlement always breeds ingratitude, boredom, and denial. Denial may be the most dangerous.

Those under the spell of these conditions will bristle at any correction or warning.

Suggest to them the possibility of America's destruction? Sacrilege. Suggest the Church slept through America's downfall, or worse, that she was complicit in her undoing? Blasphemy!

If Tozer believed many were blind and religiously confused back in his day, what would he make of the Church today? What would he say to the Church?

America's imminent destruction is now clearly in view. God is waging a war to save us. My passion is to understand what He is doing and to find my role in His miracle. Or as Tozer said, "I want to appraise the situation and see it as God sees it—to know the role of God in this day of religious confusion."

I am an evangelist. I am not a prophet. In 2012 I was minding my own business when God ordered me to write blogs about America's political situation. He told me that someone else refused to obey His call to write the blogs I wrote.

I loved the life I had before that blog. I was busy winning lost souls and seeing wonderful miracles of healings in some of our nation's worst areas.

The funny thing is that as I decried the evils of drugs and gang violence, the Church at large was blessed. But as soon as I began to expose leftist government—the worst drug and the worst gang in the inner city—I was attacked. Remember, I spent ten years reaching out on the University of California, Berkeley campus. It took no time at all for me to see how insidious socialism and Marxism truly are. These two ideologies ruin anything they touch.

However, because God was behind the blog, millions grabbed hold of its message.

Then I got a very dark sense about 2019. Apparently, Dennis Prager felt the same thing and wrote this at the beginning of 2019: "The Democratic Party and the media will do to American political life what it has done to the arts; the universities; the high schools; the Boy Scouts; race relations; religion; the happiness of so many women (misled by feminism regarding marriage and career); the moral fabric of American life (morality reduced to feelings); late-night television; mainstream Judaism, Catholicism and Protestantism; pro football; and the sexual innocence of the young: It will poison it."[2] He was painfully correct.

Now America is sinking and suffocating in a mire of God-hating ideologies. The forces on the left now seem capable of taking the law into their own hands with impunity.

So, what is God doing about all this? Since America was a miracle from the beginning and the teachings of Jesus influenced our creation, God will not let America die without mounting an astounding counterattack on evil. I call it the Godsend. This is dedicated to those who have an assignment in this Godsend.

Chapter 1

BEFORE THERE CAN BE A GREAT AWAKENING, THERE MUST BE A RUDE AWAKENING

BEFORE A GREAT AWAKENING, THERE MUST BE A RUDE awakening. The jolt the American Church needs is far greater than we know. We need a Godsend. Something outside us. Something so far beyond our imagination that we would be dumbfounded by its description.

Two things would shock us to our core: if we knew our true condition before God, and if we knew how close America is to destruction. We need a Godsend.

What does a Godsend look like? A Godsend is disruptive. It exposes falsehood. It speaks truth to power. It does not negotiate its demands. It is supernatural in its origin and execution.

A perfect clue is John the Baptist. *"There was a man sent from God, whose name was John"* (John 1:6). The Bible even calls him a Godsend!

He is not comfortable or charming. Not a soothing voice or gracious speaker. He is a wrecking ball. His looks, his message, and his demands are radical and offensive to all except *"those who hunger and thirst for righteousness"* (Matt. 5:6). He upends religion and points to a new order.

Despite all this, vast crowds march to the wilderness to be baptized and hear of the coming Messiah. A Godsend carries a message few would consider a winning message.

But what we deem a hard message may actually be the one that will ignite a soul to fall before God. Therein lies our great ignorance of both God and the yearnings of the human heart.

Millions of American Christians assume America is entitled to survival. Let me assure you, the Lord God Almighty has not cheapened His majesty to keep us alive.

Think about God. Think of the empires He has seen rise and fall. He has witnessed the destruction of many nations. He has overseen cultures that thought they would never die. Nineveh had a sign that read "the city that will always be." Nahum the prophet reminded them of the great miracle they saw with Jonah as he foretold their delayed but certain doom. God has seen delusion before. Entitlement has never stopped judgement.

America has an amazing history. We have been spared destruction again and again by divine intervention. However, something has changed. This is the first time our culture started shaking its fist at Almighty God. We have crossed over into moral unchartered waters. We have an enemy we have never faced before—ourselves.

Abraham Lincoln said: "At what point then is the approach of danger to be expected? I answer, if it ever reach us, it must spring up amongst us. It cannot come from abroad. If destruction be our lot, we must ourselves be its author and finisher. As a nation of freemen, we must live through all time or die by suicide."[1] *Suicide* is a big word.

Suicide happens when life becomes too painful. Americans are in unbearable pain. Americans feel dread. Not since Lincoln have we been this divided. As voices drown one another out, millions in the middle truly wonder how long before destruction will be our lot.

We are drowning in falsehoods. We can't trust anything we hear in the media. And no one knows how dangerous that is because it has never happened before.

Few Americans make it through a day without alcohol, a toke, a pill, powder, or a needle. For heaven's sake, our children are taking their own lives over shoes, pictures, texts, and messages on social media. Yet, few admit the direct correlation between our misery and rejection of God.

What can save us? Nothing less than a massive moral awakening.

Maybe I'm biased because I'm a part of it, but I believe the Pentecostal/Charismatic movement holds the greatest promise of catalyzing a national miracle. Specifically, because of the truth of the baptism of the Holy Spirit.

Pentecostals have had the longest unbroken move of God in history. That is until now.

This movement is now weak, disoriented, divided, and rapidly losing relevance. It needs electrode paddles applied to her faintly beating heart. We were done in by our own version of a deep state. We were infiltrated. The engine that drove Spirit-filled momentum has been replaced.

A masterstroke of Satan—decades in its construction—worked to weaken many Spirit-filled leaders. Satan fooled leaders into replacing gold with bronze.

> *And he took away the treasures of the house of the Lord and the treasures of the king's house; he took away everything. He also took away all the gold shields which Solomon had made. Then King Rehoboam made bronze shields in their place, and committed them to the hands of the captains of the guard, who guarded the doorway of the king's house* (1 Kings 14:26-27).

The devil used craftiness to steal our gold. We removed mass soul-winning through the Holy Spirit. He tossed the bone of getting a big church to drooling leaders. We replaced revival with marketing and well-oiled, business entertainment centers.

Grace is supposed to be a catalyst to holiness. A rampant new version of grace grants a license to lead a double life.

New Age nuances led many Spirit-filled Christians into out-of-Bible experiences. Never-never lands where emotional experiences and personal prophecies take supremacy over the Word of God.

The worst mistake was to stop teaching and leading people into the baptism of the Holy Spirit.

Most youth in Spirit-filled churches have never seen a miracle. The result is an entire generation who doesn't know what they believe, why they believe it, let alone possess authority to share it. They embody Judges 2:10: "*When all that generation had been gathered to their fathers, another generation arose after them who did not know the Lord nor the work which He had done for Israel.*"

Fueling our demise are the preachers who are deepening the denial instead of warning the sheep entrusted to them by the Lord. They have even created a new level of denial saying things like, "We are blessed, nothing bad is going to happen." Or they avoid addressing the national disaster altogether.

Superstar speakers claim God has not called them to confront sin. No biblical lines are drawn against the perversions that are destroying the family.

They violated their first duty to educate believers in the Word of God and lead them into the power of God. They offered nothing that would arm believers to push back on the destruction of America.

Their presentation can make you feel all warm and fuzzy inside, but it leaves you and those you love unprotected from reality—and worse, it renders you unavailable to God.

Prophets warned the Church that marriage could be destroyed, and a boy could walk in on your little girl in the school bathroom. These smiling celebrities scoffed and said it would never happen.

Today these same voices are rejecting or ignoring the new and dire warnings of the Holy Spirit that we are on the brink of losing our nation altogether. The list of things they said would never happen but did happen, grows each day. What will it take to wake us up?

God is warring to restore firepower to the movement that began in the lowly Azusa Street Mission. Rediscovering the power of the Holy Spirit holds the greatest potential to save our nation.

In this hour it is not enough to be saved and filled with the Holy Spirit—not nearly enough. Every soldier of God must know what God is doing in their time. The New Testament begins and ends with the drama of willing vessels having their lives interrupted, ruined for mortal pursuits, commissioned for great exploits, and then launched into an amazing adventure.

Knowing what God is doing in our time protects us. For years I wondered if the Word of God was contradicting itself. On the one hand, the Bible says, *"For by grace you have been saved through faith, and that not of yourselves; it is the gift of God, not of works, lest anyone should boast"* (Eph. 2:8-9). Clearly, we are not saved by works but by grace through faith.

But then Jesus said in Matthew 24:13, *"But he who endures to the end shall be saved."* Doesn't that mean that works save us? The answer is clear and wonderful. In Matthew 24, Jesus is foretelling the explosive events of the last days. He is teaching us how to live in those times. Our soul is saved from hell by grace and faith. Our lives are protected from last days' disaster by enduring—by standing and pressing into the work of God in our time.

Those who go deeper and are active in God's work receive special favor and intimacy with Christ. That protection is tied to fulfilling the very next verse: *"And this gospel of the kingdom will be preached in all the world as a witness to all the nations, and then the end will come"* (Matt. 24:14).

I am imprisoned in the reality that God is at war to save America. My passion has been to study His Word, seek His face, discern how He is waging this war, and determine my assignment in it.

I had an experience that seemed to take me from the depths of hell to the very throne of God. It jarred me and showed me the fierce war God is waging right now and how urgent it was for me to know my assignment.

At 3:00 a.m. the voice of God shook me awake. "Study the American youth culture." My assignment was not a joy. Research uncovered a world of addiction, despair, and moral confusion that was beyond my strength to absorb.

Many days of this brought me to a horror. One night, my room grew unusually dark. A stench introduced the evil presence. "I will," the evil one said. "I will have them. I will addict them. I will pervert them. I will kill them." Satan was talking about our children!

Just as suddenly, the presence of God flooded the room and swallowed the boasts of Satan, *"But I will pour out of My Spirit on them and they shall prophesy."* I was awestruck by the presence and power of God. But what really impacted me was the ferocious zeal of the Lord to save America. He is not going let this nation go down without giving the devil the fight of his life.

God is doing something to save America. He is warring to save it. Do you know how He is doing this? We are at war. If you say the name of Christ, you are in this war. That you can't see it or feel it doesn't make it any less real—or any less dangerous. The question is, do you know how God is fighting and do you know your assignment in this act of God?

Chapter 2

WHY SATAN MUST DESTROY AMERICA

S ATAN NEEDS TO DESTROY AMERICA. IT'S HIS GRAND prize. The need consumes him. He fantasizes about it. He pursues the destruction of the US with extreme prejudice and unrelenting patience.

Why do you need to know about Satan's passion to destroy America? Without this insight, you cannot muster the necessary urgency to obey God. You must know what is at stake to be willing to pay the price.

America is a firewall that prevents the one event Satan craves most: global anarchy. Anarchy is the only thing that will make the world embrace Lucifer's worldwide dictatorship.

This is why the most important goal of evil is chaos.

Marxists believe goodness magically rises out of chaos. Another group, radically opposite Marxism, also values chaos.

Karl Marx wanted socialism. But he gave up on getting it through elections. He realized that people would never vote to give up their rights. He concluded that violent revolution was essential to setting his system in place. Here's the bizarre part: Marxism and radical Islam are natural enemies. One holds that Allah—among other things—must be erased totally. The other, that Allah must be served totally. How then did Marxism and radical Islam find common ground? You got it—their mutual faith in chaos.

Here's how they both believe destroying civil order will bring something wonderful. Radical Islamists believe it will bring their messiah the Mahdi. Marxists believe it will bring "the design of the prime mover."[1]

Joel C. Rosenberg explains that "[Iran and ISIS] believe that the Mahdi will come only when the world is engulfed in chaos and carnage. They openly vow not simply to attack but to annihilate the United States and Israel. Iran and ISIS are both eager to hasten the coming of the Mahdi."[2]

According to Ludwig von Mises, "Marxism is a revolutionary doctrine. It expressly declares that the design of the prime mover will be accomplished by civil war.... The liquidation of all dissenters will establish the undisputed supremacy of the absolute eternal values. This formula for the solution of conflicts of value judgments is certainly not new. It is a device known and practiced from time immemorial. Kill the infidels! Burn the heretics! What is new is merely the fact that today it is sold to the public under the label of 'science.'"[3]

Barack Obama was the perfect fusion of this contradiction.

But Jihadists and Marxists don't know they are puppets. They live by the adage that my enemy's enemy is my friend. All the while, Satan is pulling the strings.

So how did Satan sell violent Marxist/Jihadist revolution to Americans? The first step was to hide their true intention by blurring language. George Orwell said, "When there is a gap between one's real and one's declared aims, one turns as it were instinctively to long words and exhausted idioms, like a cuttlefish squirting out ink."[4]

How often have you seen a YouTube video of a leftist college student, confronted by a simple question bursting into a flow of utterly unintelligible language?

Labels such as *homophobe, Islamophobe, sexist,* and *racist* are used to destroy careers without evidence and due process. Their new favorite is xenophobe, a time-saving slur that allows one to throw anyone who disagrees into one basket of "bigotry."

Deceptive language is how Christian values are reclassified into hatred. Ideas that are moral and trustworthy become hateful. Marriage, manhood, military service, freedom of speech, witnessing, the Bible, freedom, and even the American flag all turn into symbols of oppression.

Next, they radicalize their victims in the heat of artificial outrage. At this point they can reveal their true goal of chaos. Before long, they are acting like the very thing they claim they oppose.

This is how Berkeley—the birthplace of the free speech movement—ends up banning free speech and the American Civil Liberties Union justifies removing civil liberties. This is why radical feminists won't condemn radical Islam even with its record of brutality against women, and anti-fascists become fascists.

They will ban, boycott, and use violence for the greater good. Words can equal physical violence. "What you said felt like a punch, so I'm going to punch you."

The Bible says, *"Woe to those who call evil good, and good evil; who put darkness for light, and light for darkness; who put bitter for sweet, and sweet for bitter!"* (Isa. 5:20).

Globalism is another tool of Satan. Globalists love to say they're creating mutual economic benefit and an interconnected world. Sounds great, but it's just a front for a social prison.

No matter how beautifully the billboard reads, the ultimate product is horrifying. It's a Trojan horse. It's the scaffolding to gain worldwide control.

Just as the devil gets communists and jihadists to act in concert, he gets globalists and anarchists to work together. In this case, the contradiction is much more glaring because these two groups openly oppose each other.

Violent protestors and billionaires are working together? Unwittingly, yes. One is building the mayhem, the other is building the prison humanity will run to for shelter from the mayhem.

Love him, hate him, Trump was right. Every trade deal was slanted against America. The United Nations is a sick joke. Behind all this is a dark power. The Judeo-Christian ethic and American exceptionalism are singled out as the world's most hated values. Can you see why?

All these groups have one end in common: America must be destroyed. Either by Marxist revolution, jihad, or corporate domination.

They all have another thing in common: they all hate Trump. Trump was never supposed to happen. He disrupted their plans.

But Trump supporters must realize he was only a foot in the door—a stay of execution. He is an act of God to buy the Church time to repent and return to her rightful role in American life.

Trump is not a pastor or a moral reformer. His role is specialized and only for a season. It rests with us to seize the opening to avert disaster.

Not until you see the unbridled malice and rage of the devil toward America will you see the urgency of action and be willing to pay the price to do great exploits.

I am asking you to make an irrevocable decision to be in the middle of God's greatest acts in history. At this moment, God is selecting people and working in them for unmatched power to overcome evil. He is recruiting people to do things that are beyond comprehension. Someone is going to heed this call and do astonishing works for Christ. I must ask...why not you?

Chapter 3

EVERYONE KNOWS SOMETHING IS COMING

I N EVERY AGE SATAN UNLEASHES A WEAPON OF MASS deception. Heaven is not passive, nor surprised. God can't be fooled. He not only stays ahead of the wiles of evil, He exploits them for His own purpose.

At the approach of evil, God recruits people. He yearns to express His supremacy over evil through purified vessels. Presently God is conducting the most aggressive search for available servants in American history.

To understand what is coming we must revisit the Valley of Dry Bones.

As far as Ezekiel can see are bones—bleached dry bones. To the north, south, east and west nothing but bones. The message to the prophet is graphic: there is no life here. None.

From above the valley, the voice of the Lord thunders a question: *"Can these bones live?"* (Ezek. 37:3). Ezekiel does not answer right away. I mean, what if these are the bones of previous prophets who gave the wrong answer. He humbly says, *"Only you know"* (Ezek. 37:3 HCSB).

Then—in a first for any prophet—he is asked to prophesy something he can't imagine. What happens next is at once terrifying and glorious.

> *So I prophesied as I was commanded; and as I prophesied, there was a noise, and suddenly a rattling; and the bones came together, bone to bone. Indeed, as I looked, the sinews and the flesh came upon them, and the skin covered them over; but there was no breath in them. Also He said to me, "Prophesy to the breath, prophesy, son of man, and say to the breath, 'Thus says the Lord God: "Come from the four winds, O breath, and breathe on these slain, that they may live."'" So I prophesied as He commanded me, and breath came into them, and they lived, and stood upon their feet, an exceedingly great army* (Ezekiel 37:7-10).

Israel has no hope. That's the first point. Verse 11: *"Then He said to me, 'Son of man, these bones are the whole house of Israel. They indeed say, "Our bones are dry, our hope is lost, and we ourselves are cut off!"'"*

The second point is the major point: God will come out of nowhere. When everything is past hope, He will restore life. Why? So that we may know He is God and He alone has done it. Hold on to that truth.

God always begins with a secret promise. He knows His servants and brands them with that secret. Amos 3:7 says, *"Surely the*

Lord God does nothing, unless He reveals His secret to His servants the prophets."

This creates a prisoner of hope. Ezekiel saw the molecule-scrambling vision of bones restored to life. God told him a secret. He is marked for life. He is separated from humanity by a promise.

Twin emotions collide within him. He must carry the prediction of something that is at once unimaginable yet undeniable.

What God is warring to do in America is like the Valley of Dry Bones. It is impossible. It must bring life where no life exists. It happens in a way that no man can take credit. Only God can do a thing like this. But everyone knows something is coming.

I do this test in many places where I preach. I ask the audience a simple question: How many of you have either received a word from the Lord directly, or from a credible source, that God is going to pour out His Spirit in your area?

Hands go up everywhere—not just all over the room, but in every city. It usually stuns the audience how many have received the same message. But it begs another question: How can all these people be wrong? We can discount some of it to emotion and some of it to hopefulness. But after that we are still left with a remarkable phenomenon. God is saying the same thing to a whole lot of people.

Even more intriguing are the detailed descriptions and similarities. Many speak of deep repentance, holiness, mighty miracles, judgement on some, blessings on others. But, to a person, they are convinced that God is sending strong medicine because this is America's last chance.

But if God is sending a radical cure, it can only mean a radical sickness is in progress. If you reject the severity of the sickness, you are also rejecting the cure. Now let me tell you how I became a prisoner of hope.

In 1978 I quit the ministry. Not just any ministry either. I was leading a student movement at the University of California, Berkeley. It was at the height of the Jesus movement. Some of the things God did were so amazing I still can't write about them.

Many (some say thousands) were converted. Only God knows the exact number. An equal number testified to dramatic healings. Those signs and wonders cracked open the campus.

A paralyzing sense of closure came over me. I couldn't shake the feeling that this amazing era had run its course. I hit an emotional brick wall.

How bizarre to witness such a breakthrough and yet feel it was all over. I got to the point where I felt I had to get out of Berkeley. Fast!

I even wrote out my resignation. I looked at God and said, "I quit." He said, "Before you quit, go upstairs and pray." I said, "No, because I know what You are going to do. You're going make me another promise." Finally, I went upstairs and prayed.

After a violent season of prayer—that involved tossing furniture—a calm overshadowed me. Then came the still small voice, "I will pour out My Spirit on San Francisco and the world will look and wonder." Now I was truly angry! I screamed: "This is impossible. It cannot happen! If this is true, I demand an infallible sign now!"

Instantly, the phone beside me started ringing.

I stared at the phone. I finally answered it. "Mario? This is Bob Dylan calling." I am unable to register what is happening. Why is the most famous folk singer in the world calling me on the phone?

He had met Christ. He was going to do his first Christian concert in San Francisco. He knew it was going to be a volatile situation and wanted someone to intercede backstage while he performed.

We talked a little more and then just as we were about to hang up, he asked me, "Mario, did God tell you He was going to pour out His Spirit on San Francisco?" Losing my breath and about to faint, I said, "Yes." To which he responded, "Well Mario, He is going to pour out His Spirit on San Francisco."

Did I just hear Bob Dylan repeat the exact same words the Lord spoke to me moments before? I am once again branded by a promise.

The promise kept growing in me until one day I knew it was time to invade San Francisco. I found myself looking across the desk of the manager of the most famous arena in San Francisco—an arena with sixteen thousand seats. "How much will it cost to rent the main auditorium for seven days?" His rock-bottom price was $120,000 plus seven dollars per car to park.

It was in that moment that I discovered what the promise of God had done in me. The old me would have walked out in the face of such impossibility. The new me, well, reacted differently. I jumped to my feet. I ripped back the curtains of his office. I pointed to the projects across the street. I was angry. I began yelling at him.

I pointed at the tenement housing across the street. "Look at those projects! There's addiction, violence, and hopeless despair in there. You, sir, need to start giving something back!"

Realizing what I had just said, I was prepared to be thrown out. He, on the other hand, realizing what I had just said, slumped in his chair and looked down. His eyes moistened, and he began to write. With a look I knew could cost him his job, he cut $60,000 off the price.

We amassed one of the largest Christian outreaches San Francisco had ever seen. Bob Johnson and his team led a remarkable ministry among the homeless, addicts, and prostitutes all over the city.

But every week we ran out of money. And every week a miracle would reinstate our mission. Mario Murillo Ministries had drained its savings over and over again. Then disaster struck.

I was sitting in a café courtyard. It was six days before opening night at the Cow Palace. I got the call. We owed $100,000. I had four days to raise it or the event will be canceled. We had $1,263.23. It was over. The promise was an elaborate and cruel joke.

If you ever want to empty an outdoor café, throw your head back and start crying out in tongues. I didn't dare open my eyes.

Meanwhile, inside the café a businessman named Joe Little was eating with his wife and young daughters. We had met six months prior at Phoenix First Assembly. I found out he lived in the Bay Area, and I had given him my card.

A wall separated their section of the restaurant and the courtyard where my meltdown was scaring people. He couldn't see or hear me.

"I don't know why" Joe said to his wife, "but I feel I must call Mario Murillo and give him money." He got up and headed across the restaurant to get my card out of his glove compartment. Then he saw me.

When I finally had the courage to open my eyes, Joe was sitting across from me with tears running down his face. "Mario Murillo, you scare me to death! The Lord showed me you need a lot of money." I looked him in the eye and said, "The Lord is right!"

It took all my willpower not to tell him an amount. I just sat there wanting this to be totally God. What he said next still hits my spirit as if it just happened. He said, "Would $100,000 help you?"

We paid our debt the next day.

Fourteen thousand people flowed into the arena on opening night. My sermon was extremely simple. I quoted Luke 19:5, *"And when Jesus came to the place, He looked up and saw him, and said to him, 'Zacchaeus, make haste and come down, for today I must stay at your house.'"*

A thick blanket of the Holy Spirit covered the crowd as I started my appeal to come to Jesus. Something only God can do started happening. Chains began falling off the homeless, gang members, prostitutes, and addicts. Souls flowed together forming a river of humanity streaming its way forward to be set free.

First there was a collective gasp, a momentary silence, and then a roar of praise when the Christians realized this was actually happening in San Francisco. They say two thousand people came forward. Only God knows the real number.

Standing there watching this astounding moment, I felt a chill of how close I came to missing this moment. I thought about the amazing fact of Bob Dylan calling at just the right moment, with just the right word. And Joe Little stepping in right on time.

I thought, "This is what God promised. He poured out His Spirit on this notorious city." Then the voice of the Lord said, "This is still not it." Still not it? What does that mean?

Today I understand that the promised outpouring in San Francisco was just one of many. But His coming event is not just a blessing; it is a terrifying occurrence. We must understand what God means to create.

What He means to create—when He finds true surrender—is stunning. He will imbue His own with power to perform notable miracles, power to speak with irresistible force, and power to transfer the wealth of the wicked into the Gospel. Ready or not, it is coming.

When you write a book, you should know what it is about. I know what I am trying to tell you. Spirit-filled believers live in an unfulfilled destiny. God keeps that destiny ready. The Lord wants us overtaken by dual emotions: unshakable expectation that something is coming and reverential fear that we can miss it.

Chapter 4

WHY THE TIME
IS NOW

I F THAT WASN'T IT THEN WHAT IS IT? I MEAN WHAT DOES a national awakening look like? There are reasons we don't know. Partly because we can't imagine what it would take to pull America out of the grave she is digging for herself. And partly because God has hidden it. But we have a serious problem.

The Spirit-filled Church has rewarded men for getting good at things they're not supposed to be doing. In many respects, the outward appearance of our movement is indeed impressive. We have eloquent life coaches dazzling millions. We have sparkling campuses knit together by the latest technology. We have money. Well, at least they do.

We are highly organized. We have our finger on the pulse of social trends. We are muscle bound with administration and efficiency. But we have organized the Holy Spirit right out of our operation. We have even perfected the art of orchestrating the supernatural.

We have big screens, skinny jeans, and fog machines. What we don't have is a towering move of God. What does not thunder forth from our pulpits is truth—truth that convicts and transforms—truth spoken by a broken, loving vessel that is unconcerned with popularity.

American preachers used to be famous for being reformers and agents of change. Now they are famous for being performers who have agents.

E. M. Bounds said, "What the Church needs to-day is not more machinery or better, not new organizations or more and novel methods, but men whom the Holy Ghost can use—men of prayer, men mighty in prayer. The Holy Ghost does not flow through methods, but through men. He does not come on machinery, but on men. He does not anoint plans, but men—men of prayer."[1]

We are very good at what we do. But what good is that if it's not what we are supposed to be doing? Worst of all, we are doing it as America sinks. That makes us the best party going on the deck of the Titanic.

For this book to do anyone any good, it must pierce the heart of the reader with this single truth: we lost something, and we better get it back.

There is a growing number among us who are grieved and yet full of expectancy. They claim that nothing we are seeing in churches today approaches what we will see. They say it's coming, and no one can stop it. The locomotive of destiny is barreling toward us. Its carries precious cargo: a mighty outpouring of the Holy Spirit.

They see millions of lost souls swept into the Kingdom of God in one righteous tidal wave. A vast army of youth full of love, power, and the Holy Spirit will form virtually overnight. Satan will suffer at the hands of armor-piercing Christianity—Christianity that penetrates culture and reforms it. But are they right? Let's find out.

It's 1906 in Los Angeles. William Seymour agrees to rent a dingy horse stable at 312 Azusa Street for eight dollars a month and begins revival meetings. A movement springs out those meetings. Today it claims seven hundred million followers.

Nine days after the Azusa Street revival began, an earthquake destroys San Francisco. It topples more than twenty-eight thousand buildings. Two hundred thousand residents are instantly homeless. More than three thousand people are killed.

The public believes it's the end of the world. To the saints four hundred miles south in the Azusa Street Mission, this is a sign that Jesus is about to return. They are gripped with soul-winning fervor. They paper Los Angeles with pamphlets warning people to repent because Christ's return is imminent. They take trains to San Francisco to minister to the victims of the quake.

It's a time of mass rubble and revival. Awakenings do not begin in times of enlightened morality, prosperity, and peace. They come when humanity writhes in the depths of depravity. They arrive in the shadow of wars and convulsions in nature.

They come when society has gorged itself in pleasure and drained itself in dark pursuits. Revivals come to those most cruelly vexed by the culture. The brunt of cultural change always falls on the backs of youth. That is why they often begin with them.

But let's turn our attention to a ten-year-old boy who went to the Azusa Street Mission.

His name was A. C. Valdez. He spent years in the Azusa Street Revival. He went on to preach miracle tent revivals up and down California. His crusade in San Bernardino transformed Demos Shakarian, who founded the Full Gospel Business Men's Fellowship International.

But for all the glory Valdez witnessed at Azusa Street, he kept insisting something bigger was coming. This prediction burned in him the rest of his days. Here's how he once described it:

> All the electrifying adjectives in the dictionary shaken together, pressed down and running over will not begin to describe the soon-to-come, greatest outpouring of the Holy Spirit of all times—what the Bible calls "the latter rain." You are going to see lay members carry out an amazing ministry through gifts of the Holy Spirit. There will be wholesale cures of "incurable" conditions, healings of the blind, deaf, dumb, and handicapped, and creative miracles that will strain the imagination. For those born without eyes ears, fingers arms, or legs—or those who have lost them through disease or accidents—God will make new ones. Many astonishing miracles will happen to bring on an international Christian breakthrough.

Rereading these words doesn't make them any easier to absorb. I know because I have tried.

Why can't Pentecostal/Charismatic people believe this kind of awakening is possible? The answer oozes out of everything we do. We are in the grip of a sophisticated unbelief—an unbelief and defeatism that permeates our programs and our message.

Why would we have assembled all these working parts for the Church if we believed the Holy Spirit was enough? Why would we have severely redacted our preaching if we believed the Gospel was the power of God to everyone?

So, I must turn the tables on those who question the possibility of a Godsend. No one can present proof that there is something in the American culture that can stop God. The songwriter who said, "His truth is marching on," was more than right

Impossible you say? Admit our youth are in the worst moral condition in American history. Admit that church attendance among young people has never been this low. Admit that never have so many claimed to be atheists—never have they expressed such widespread anger toward churches. Never have we seen such derision and hostility toward the teachings of Christ. And yet, I will tell you none of these things can prevent a youth awakening.

I want to show you that the very things we say make it impossible actually play into God's hands. In fact, we do not need deep prophetic words or blazing encounters with God to see the natural factors that could indeed catalyze an awakening in America.

THE HURRICANE FACTOR

Scientists predict hurricanes by detecting the opposite of a hurricane. They see air pressure falling creating a vacuum over the ocean. Warm air rises and creates a low-pressure area. They know nature always rushes in to fill a void.

When university professors spiritually starve students, they think they are churning out atheists. Instead, they may be creating future revivalists. Their push to erase Judeo-Christian values does not remove the need for God. When one suppresses spiritual hunger, they can actually intensify the hunger.

This also explains why so many American revivals have started on college campuses. The Jesus movement is the definitive example of this. In the 1960s free love, psychedelic drugs, eastern religion, witchcraft, and rebellion ruled the day. It got so bad *Time* magazine asked, "Is God dead?"[2] The moral revolution that ensued—saving millions—came out of the blue and without warning. I know because I saw it.

This hurricane effect is described in Psalm 119:126 which says, *"It is time for You to act, O Lord, for they have regarded Your law as void."* That void is in our children. The promise to fill that void came straight from Christ: *"Blessed are those who hunger and thirst for righteousness, for they shall be filled"* (Matt. 5:6).

THE "SAUL OF TARSUS" FACTOR

How can our youth be nearing a spiritual revolution? They are going to extremes with drugs, violence, and perversion? They are wildly embracing socialism and protesting madly. Strangely enough, their bizarre behavior is itself the sign.

Acts 26:14 tells us that Jesus said to Saul of Tarsus: *"it is hard for you to kick against the goads."* Christ had been dealing with Saul for some time. The words and works of Jesus haunted Saul. Jesus and Saul were about the same age, and Saul was often in places where Jesus taught.

To *"kick against the goads"* was a common expression found in both Greek and Latin literature. Everyone in that day knew this referred to farmers using a sharp pointed stick to goad a stubborn ox into motion. He is fighting his destiny. Jesus's analogy is perfect. The ox wants to go one way, but the sharp stick is goading him another way.

Saul's destiny kept prodding him, and he reacted by becoming more violent and zealous, kicking against the goad of his destiny. By destroying the Church, he could kill the frightening work of God inside him.

Is that what many of our youth are doing now? The more they are goaded toward their destiny, the more bizarre and extreme they behave. Are they approaching the road to Damascus?

"SATAN OVERPLAYING HIS HAND"

According to the Journal of the American Medical Association, forty million Americans used one or more psychiatric drugs.[3]

Fifty percent of Americans experience significant loneliness.[4]

According to Najja Parker, the more social media you use, the lonelier you feel.[5]

For the first time since 1963 the life expectancy of Americans has declined two years in a row. The *British Medical Journal* looked into a broader cause behind the decline: despair.[6]

Satan is taking an incalculable emotional toll on Americans. If Lucifer truly wanted to fill hell, you'd think he'd make everyone rich and content. Instead, he grinds people. He makes them miserable and plunges them into despair. In the process he drives his victims to cry out to God for deliverance.

First Peter 5:8 says, *"Be sober, be vigilant; because your adversary the devil walks about like a roaring lion, seeking whom he may devour."* Satan sabotages his own plans because of his hatred. Doesn't Satan realize this will drive people to Jesus? Sure, he knows. He just can't help himself. He only knows he has to devour.

In our tent crusades in the inner city it is shocking how easily lost souls charge the front to be saved and delivered. I have not seen it like this before...not even in the Jesus movement.

The "It's God's Time" Factor

If God says it is time who can stop him? In Acts 1:7 Jesus says, *"It is not for you to know the times or dates the Father has set by his own authority"* (NIV). This confirms that times for events are set by God.

But the factors I have set before you are also a reason for God to correct us. He has the right to say, *"How dare you ignore the factors that come before an awakening?"* Jesus put it this way:

> *Whenever you see a cloud rising out of the west, immediately you say, "A shower is coming"; and so it is. And when you see the south wind blow, you say, "There will be hot weather"; and there is. Hypocrites! You can discern the face of the sky and of the earth, but how is it you do not discern this time?* (Luke 12:54-56)

California is not a lost cause. It is in fact one of the most prepared fields anywhere in the world. All four factors are at work there. Apocalyptic fires, bizarre extremes of behavior, radical opposition to God, and massive emotional problems point to a hurricane.

Repentance in our time looks like this: We abandon methods that while good, would be a drag on revival. We examine the crimes we have committed against the Holy Spirt and we forsake them. We end our theological apology tour. We look the culture right in the eye and say, "I know you will hate me and say I am judgmental, but what I am about to tell you will bring life—life like you never imagined." And we prepare.

SECTION II

MODERN CRIMES AGAINST THE HOLY SPIRIT

THE SIMPLE FACT THAT JESUS WEPT OVER JERUSALEM for missing the hour of their visitation proves they should have known. Why didn't they? How could they miss something so basic to their faith and survival?

One answer is, they were betrayed by their teachers. Jesus marveled at Nicodemus and said, *"Are you the teacher of Israel, and do not know these things?"* (John 3:10)

Megachurches boom, yet on their watch we have had our greatest moral decline. This says leaders have learned to do church without the Holy Spirit. The rampant fascination with false doctrine and emotional extremes are also products of a movement that has lost its relationship to the Holy Spirit.

Our crimes become more glaring when we consider the magnitude of the original mandate Jesus gave regarding the Holy Spirit. John 16:13-15 says:

> *However, when He, the Spirit of truth, has come, He will guide you into all truth; for He will not speak*

on His own authority, but whatever He hears He will speak; and He will tell you things to come. He will glorify Me, for He will take of what is Mine and declare it to you. All things that the Father has are Mine. Therefore I said that He will take of Mine and declare it to you.

He will take everything Jesus has and show it to us. We can't learn it outside of Him. He is our relevance to the world and the organizer of our church operations. He decodes the culture and shows us how to advance. He is the architect and general of our outreach to the world. It falls to Him to lead, train, empower, and equip us.

No matter how cherished or effective a method seems, once it is revealed to be outside the Holy Spirit, it must be abandoned. We cannot prepare for the Godsend without first facing and forsaking our crimes against the Holy Spirit.

Chapter 5

THE CRIME OF CHURCH GROWTH WITHOUT THE HOLY SPIRIT

*"I consider that the chief dangers which
confront the coming century will be...religion
without the Holy Ghost, Christianity without
Christ, forgiveness without repentance,
salvation without regeneration, politics
without God and heaven without hell."*
—WILLIAM BOOTH, founder of The Salvation Army

THE HOLY SPIRIT WAS NOT SENT MERELY TO MAKE UP FOR Jesus leaving. He was sent to multiply, exponentially, Jesus's impact on the earth. He was sent to run the operation. He was the wisdom, the power, the inventiveness, and the force for church growth and world evangelism. I will say more about this later.

Instead of trusting the Holy Spirit, Spirit-filled leaders sat in a seminar and were enticed by the idea of a big church. What they gave away is a treasure that can't be measured. What they gained is a horrendous counterfeit—the kind you get anytime you make a deal with the devil.

The enemy tricked Spirit-filled preachers. What followed was a devastating waste of time, energy, and resources. Worst of all, the Church of God was cowed off the front lines when America needed her most.

They bought a counterfeit kingdom. The scheme promised grandiose results but in practice only produced weaker Christians and decreasing influence in America. It was fool's gold.

This generation of pastors gave in to the temptation that Jesus overcame in AD 30.

Remember when the Holy Spirit drove Jesus into the wilderness to be tempted of Satan? Consider how much time the evil one had to prepare to lay a trap for Christ. He processed millions of options before settling on three temptations.

However, it is the second temptation that matters most to us. The Bible says in Luke 4:5-8:

> *Then the devil, taking Him up on a high mountain, showed Him all the kingdoms of the world in a moment of time. And the devil said to Him, "All this authority I will give You, and their glory; for this has been delivered to me, and I give it to whomever I wish. Therefore, if You will worship before me, all will be Yours." And Jesus answered and said to him, "Get behind Me, Satan! For it is written, 'You shall worship the Lord your God, and Him only you shall serve.'"*

A casual observer will think this was the easiest temptation. Christ came from indescribable glory. How could the puny kingdoms of the world impress the One who had for eons received the adoration of countless angels and innumerable worlds?

The power of this temptation is seduction—seduction to save the world without going to the cross. It's a two-edged sword. One side touches Christ's fathomless love for mankind. The other touches His humanity—the side that agonizes over the inevitable torture and slow death on the cross. In Gethsemane, with blood sweating from His forehead, His humanity would ask if the cup could pass from Him. But His divinity would again prevail: *"Not My will, but Yours be done"* (Luke 22:42).

Satan believed he could create a compromised Christ where the world would be half saved—which is to say, not saved at all. What a victory for you and me when Jesus said, *"Get behind Me, Satan! For it is written, 'You shall worship the Lord your God, and Him only you shall serve'"* (Luke 4:8).

But modern Spirit-filled preachers fell for the same temptation. They fell for it with infinitely less bait than the bait Jesus was offered. We're not talking about all the kingdoms of the world, just one—the kingdom of a big church.

The devil presented the temptation to a half-starved, exhausted Christ in the wilderness. Modern Spirit-filled pastors were tempted in a church-growth seminar. They were enticed by the idea of a megachurch. A celebrity pastor promised, "If you follow my system for church growth, you too will have a church like mine."

I might understand how a non-Pentecostal pastor could be tempted, but I am baffled by a preacher who has been baptized in the Holy Spirit—who has seen the power of God at work—putting aside the move of God to go after sheer numbers.

Scot McKnight, professor of New Testament at Northern Seminary, asks, "What is wrong with 'marketing' the Church? If the essence of evangelism is declaring good news and 'persuasion' of its truth—both in dependence on the Spirit and in the use of everything we can muster—and if marketing is about persuasion, and if there are commonalities between all acts of persuasion, what is the distinction between Church persuasion and marketing persuasion?"[1]

The distinction between those persuasions is night and day. Paul said in First Corinthians 2:4, *"And my speech and my preaching were not with persuasive words of human wisdom, but in demonstration of the Spirit and of power."* Paul knew human marketing, was skilled in it, and rejected it.

Paul understood what Jesus meant in John 16:13, *"However, when He, the Spirit of truth, has come, He will guide you into all truth; for He will not speak on His own authority, but whatever He hears He will speak; and He will tell you things to come."*

The Holy Spirit is in charge of church growth. Period. If the sharpest mind of the first century knew to lay aside human marketing in favor of surrender to the Holy Spirit, what is our excuse?

Jesus said the Spirit would lead into all truth. Does that cover how to grow a church, how to make disciples, and how to penetrate a culture?

We have to trust that Jesus meant what He said. If we do, the conclusion is plain: church growth is not, as McKnight said, "the use of everything we can muster." It is a matter of everything we can surrender.

The Church doesn't need to seek out commonalities of persuasion in order to convince a lost generation. As a matter of fact, the Spirit Himself is the convincer. *"And when he is come, he will convince the world of sin, and of justice, and of judgment"* (John 16:8 DRA).

These preachers returned from the seminar dazzled by the prospect of a big church. But, like Samson, in Judges 16:20, they knew not that the Spirit had departed from their endeavors.

These preachers either didn't feel His departure, or they drowned the feeling by repeating over and over that it is all for the greater good. They accepted the offer that Jesus rejected. They didn't have any idea who they were talking to when they said, "Yeah, I'll take that kingdom you're offering."

The cost is always the same: leave the cross out. You will only half save them—which is to say you won't save them at all. Such a pastor must learn to get joy from hollow victories. They must submerge their convictions, no matter how much it hurts. Keep telling yourself it's all for the "greater good."

Look away! One of your reprogrammed ushers just broke the heart of a true saint. "Don't raise your hands in worship! We don't do that anymore...it offends the people we are trying to reach." Keep telling yourself that statement even makes sense.

Don't listen to yourself preaching. Your sermons remove the active ingredient—the transforming power of the cross. You are creating people who may like Christ but will never be Christlike.

Smile through the shame of your silence. The talk-show host just asked you about hell and marriage between a man and a woman. You meekly mutter a lie, "God hasn't called me to preach on that."

Stop quoting "negative" Bible verses. Stop teaching the Bible verse by verse. Stop explaining Christian values. Leave the sheep unarmed and unprotected from the dizzying changes in the culture. Don't tell them how to vote or what biblical marriage is. Don't tell them how to give an answer to a perverse generation, just give them an out-of-context interpretation of "judge not" to get off the hook.

It was inevitable that something horrendous would happen. The result was catastrophic. Believers could not stand against the tide of immorality and they had no convictions or discernment and no way to counter the Left's war on the Bible.

The church-growth experts said folks would like us better. My home state of California is littered with counterfeit kingdoms built by Spirit-filled pastors. On their watch, California has declared war on Christianity.

Is it fair to implicate attraction churches in the moral decline of America? Charles Finney said, "If Satan rules in our halls of legislation, the pulpit is responsible for it. If our politics become so corrupt that the very foundations of our government are ready to fall away, the pulpit is responsible for it."[2]

No doubt the advocates of the attraction church model will cry foul. But they can't have it both ways. They are the ones who extolled the virtues of these church-growth models to fix things. Fix what?

We have four times the number of atheists we had in 1991. Our campuses are intellectual echo chambers with youth scared of opposing views. Morals have fallen faster, further, and harder than at any time in American history. America is suicidal and addicted.

When the Church in America left the Holy Spirit, America left the Church. Is that just a coincidence?

If the big church growth model can't fix the only thing that needs fixing, what is the point?

But there is another cost that can't even be quantified: this model discouraged the righteous pastor. Unable to compete with large screens, skinny jeans, and fog machines, men and women of God who stayed true to the Word of God suffered discouragement.

Christians were herded from a lot of smaller churches into bigger regional churches. It's like Amazon. Amazon did not increase the number of people who buy things, it only changed where they buy it by making it more convenient and lowering the cost. Thousands of brick and mortar stores closed because of Amazon.

Every seven days, one hundred churches close in the United States—six thousand a year![3] Some of that is because believers left one church for another church that, like Amazon, was more convenient and cost less. They were accountable to a pastor, but now they can hide in a crowd and get out quicker.

Church growth advocates love to talk about creating a wider on-ramp for non-Christians. In practice, it appears they mostly created an exit ramp for the uncommitted Christian. In fact, the overall number of Americans claiming to be Christian has dropped. Did they just rearrange furniture?

Since they left the Holy Spirit behind, it was inevitable that carnality would take hold and take them further and further into carnality.

God is warning us from the Book of Amos. The central altar of God had been replaced by rogue altars. These altars mingled pagan superstition and Jewish tradition. They left the Bible out of their worship. They did it then for the same reason it is done today: to gain wider acceptance. Their version of wanting a big church.

Hear the word of the Lord:

> *"Hear and testify against the house of Jacob," says the Lord God, the God of hosts, "That in the day I punish Israel for their transgressions, I will also visit destruction on the altars of Bethel; and the horns of the altar shall be cut off and fall to the ground. I will destroy the winter house along with the summer house; the houses of ivory shall perish, and the great houses shall have an end," says the Lord* (Amos 3:13-15).

Two years later, an earthquake destroyed everything Amos targeted. Matthew Henry said something chilling about these verses: "If men will not destroy idolatrous altars, God will, and those with them that had them in veneration."[4]

This applies to every church in America that has erected idolatrous altars. This is also a warning to all who would destroy the miracle of liberty that came from our Declaration of Independence and our Constitution.

If the Church will not rise up and speak, God will turn even nature against us to spare America.

Look at our rogue altars. Worship leaders prance church stages in revealing outfits. They see nothing wrong with it. They even teach that the body is a beautiful thing and if you have bad thoughts, it's in your mind. The Bible disagrees. Proverbs 7:10 says, *"And there a woman met him, with the attire of a harlot, and a crafty heart."* The New International Version says, *"dressed like a prosti- tute."* If you don't want the label, don't wear the uniform.

We have pastors getting drunk with their staff after church. They began by justifying wine and then moved on to hard liquor. They justify it with grace teaching from beyond the Bible. Did grace drive you to drink?

Both acts come from another wickedness—abandoning the Bible. The Bible is gone as a standard. It is no longer regarded as the Word of God. It got in the way of church growth.

Meanwhile, out in the world, a confederation of teachers desires to teach your child how to use sex toys—and to get them to experiment with gender. They have drag queens reading stories to children in our libraries.

They have already systemically changed California into a sep- arate nation, and without a miracle, the beliefs will spread like cancer to the rest of the United States. Yet California is home to some of the largest megachurches in America.

The ideas and values that created America are under heavy attack. It is not a physical war. This is in the spirit world. Demonic engines drive this agenda. That makes the carnal churches special villains in the eyes of God.

Scantily clad women on stage and inebriated ministers are no longer just a matter of hypocrisy and carnality; it is blasphemy. When they—who are supposed to be leading the charge against darkness—instead, help advance the darkness, they are traitors. And I would argue that it is high treason because it aids and abets the destruction of our freedoms.

No one is better equipped to break the curse than the Church. Conservatives can only do so much. Your favorite commentator can only do so much. Ben Shapiro and Jordan Peterson can only accomplish a part of what we need.

It is left to the apostles, prophets, teachers, pastors, and evangelists to take up the mantle for this hour. But to our great horror, instead of purifying themselves for the battle of their lives, instead of seeking holy fire to combat the evil, many are gorging on cheap grace, testing the limits of decency, and falling into dangerous addictions.

People point out that these entertainment churches "produce musicals as good as Broadway" or "they give the average person hope." But these achievements ring hollow. In a simpler time they would be impressive. Not today.

This is no time for entertainment. This is no time for mild cures. Society's condition changed the rules. A demon-possessed culture needs a Church with power to cast out devils. A culture reeling with unimaginable addictions needs a Church where the baptism of the Holy Spirit and the fire of God are plainly presented.

In a time of mass murder, mass suicide, of hurricanes, floods, and fire, is it time for pastors to parade wealth and grant these mild cures?

Haggai asked another painful question: *"Is it time for you yourselves to dwell in your paneled houses, and this temple to lie in ruins?"* (Hag. 1:4).

The modern application for this is simple: Pastor, are you building a personal empire, or the Kingdom of God? Will you allow America to go down in flames while you live in a bubble of false victory?

Not only a false victory but a draining one at that. The vigorous and unending work generated by a human-fueled attraction church never ends. It burns up staff, it exhausts morale with no end in sight. Moreover, the audience gets worse from the constant pampering. Their appetite increases even as their commitment decreases.

Instead of becoming a black hole of maintenance, the Spirit-driven Church enjoys momentum. The Holy Spirit deepens the congregation even as He widens its impact. The leadership is freed up to seek God and deliver the results of that communion to the people.

The Pentecostal movement has grown to over seven hundred million adherents because of raw power demonstrated in unapologetic preaching. The hallmarks were the baptism in the Holy Spirit, which created witnesses and miracles that verified the preaching. A church of even ten thousand members is a paltry result beside the millions reached by true Pentecost.

Here's the bottom line: Wanting numbers forced the preaching to dumb down the audience. Light, inspirational themes replaced biblical foundations of faith. The seed of truth was never planted deeply. People worshipped quickly and were superficially amused by God.

The result was catastrophic. Believers could not stand against the tide of immorality and they had no convictions or discernment to see the need to vote or even how to vote.

There is nothing wrong with a big church—that got big for the right reasons and by the right power.

If we can truly confess that babble has replaced the Bible, that self-enhancement has replaced self-denial, that marketing has replaced miracles, and unconditionally surrender to the Holy Spirit, God will turn our churches into fire-breathing, nation-changing powerhouses.

Chapter 6

THE CRIME OF NOT JUDGING RIGHTEOUSLY

THE TELEVISION HOST LOOKED AT THE PREACHER AND asked, "What is your opinion on homosexuality?" His instant response was, "My opinion does not matter. But here's what the Word of God says." Then he quoted the Bible.

The host's gotcha question turned into a something unexpected. Instead of dealing with the preacher and labeling him a bigot, they were forced to deal with their hostility toward the Bible—something they didn't want the public to see.

What this preacher did was right on more levels than meets the eye. It also exposes one of the greatest and costliest crimes against the Holy Spirit. This is a crime that contributed greatly to America's moral landslide. Abusing the words, "Judge not."

It is one of the most abused quotes of Jesus: *"Judge not, that you be not judged. For with what judgment you judge, you will be judged; and with the measure you use, it will be measured back to you"* (Matt. 7:1-2).

Many celebrity preachers claim this verse is directing us to speak life and never tell people they are wrong. In some of their growth manuals they direct pastors never to use "negative" scriptures or even to avoid quoting the Bible.

Often, Christian speakers and singers are interviewed on talk shows and deflect questions on the existence of hell, Jesus as the only way to salvation, abortion, and same-sex marriage. They say, "Jesus told me not to judge." Funny thing, the Left agrees with that.

What both the Christian celebrity and the Left are actually claiming is that Jesus said we are never to tell anyone they are wrong. This is an odd conclusion for the Left since they find fault in almost everything. But they have since cleared up the confusion by telling us, "We can judge but you can't."

If Jesus meant that we are never to tell anyone they are wrong, then there is a big problem. That is impossible to obey. If you tell me not to judge, you are telling me I am wrong, ergo you are judging. When any popular preacher refuses to answer hard questions by saying, "Jesus told me not to judge," he is judging his brethren. He is throwing them under the bus. He is distancing himself from preachers who draw moral conclusions from the Bible. He is saying they are disobeying Jesus.

The only way you can ever obey this command is by never speaking. Any firm opinion infers that others are wrong. Check your own reaction to what I just wrote. Some of you just read this and thought, "Mario, you are wrong about this." Bingo!

The problem goes much deeper. If Jesus is telling us never to tell anyone they are wrong, then there is a glaring contradiction. He goes on in that chapter to call people dogs, pigs, ravenous wolves, and even says His audience is evil.

Do not give what is holy to the dogs; nor cast your pearls before swine, lest they trample them under their feet, and turn and tear you in pieces (Matthew 7:6).

If you then, being evil, know how to give good gifts to your children, how much more will your Father who is in heaven give good things to those who ask Him! (Matthew 7:11)

Beware of false prophets, who come to you in sheep's clothing, but inwardly they are ravenous wolves (Matthew 7:15).

Clearly, Jesus means something else. So, what does He mean?

Matthew 7 is the final installment of Christ's Sermon on the Mount. Here Jesus is continuing His rebuke of the Pharisees. They have set themselves up as authorities and have claimed their traditions to be equal to God's Law. Matthew 15:9 says, *"And in vain they worship Me, teaching as doctrines the commandments of men."*

The Pharisees were playing God. They were also overruling the Law and impersonating officers of the court. In rebuking them, He was not just saying "Judge not," He was saying, "Don't be a judge."

Do not impersonate an officer of the court by rendering verdicts—verdicts that are your opinion and not the Law or the Word of God. You have no authority to do this. Hence the preacher said, "My opinion does not matter, but here's what the Word of God says."

When a preacher stands in the pulpit and calls out sin, it must never be a private opinion. He or she must faithfully pass on the verdict of God and do it in fear and trembling.

This also explains the consequence of judging in verse 2, *"For with what judgment you judge, you will be judged; and with the measure you use, it will be measured back to you."* Impersonating a cop has dire consequences, how much more impersonating God.

Jesus warns us not to assume God's prerogative to condemn the guilty. This was never meant as a license to stop discerning truth from error. Jesus does not oppose correcting people—only offering correction in the wrong spirit. We must not sit in the judgment seat to make our word a law to everybody.

What should be our attitude in offering correction? Not only does Jesus explain that, here we find proof—when our spirit is right—of our duty to bring correction. Matthew 7:4-5: *"Or how can you say to your brother, 'Let me remove the speck from your eye'; and look, a plank is in your own eye? Hypocrite! First remove the plank from your own eye, and then you will see clearly to remove the speck from your brother's eye."*

If our first instinct is to see faults in others first—if we think they have the plank and we have the speck—if we sit in a service hearing a powerful word and think, "I wish John could have heard this; man, he needs it," we are in error. If our instinct is not to check our own heart first, watch out! Jonathan Edwards said, "A true saint is suspicious of nothing more than his own heart."

We are ready to bring correction when we have first allowed God to correct us. We are ready to bring correction when the heart of the Father for a sinner pervades our disgust at their sin.

When we look at a homeless addict and see how Satan has disfigured a life through addiction—a life that otherwise might have been beautiful—and we feel the tragedy, then we are ready to offer life.

Such was the masterful moment in *A Christmas Carol*. Scrooge had judged the poor—calling them "surplus population." But then the Spirit of Christmas Present showed him two children:

> From the foldings of its robe it brought two children, wretched, abject, frightful, hideous, miserable. They knelt down at its feet, and clung upon the outside of its garment.
>
> "Oh, Man! Look here! Look, look, down here!" exclaimed the Ghost.
>
> They were a boy and a girl. Yellow, meagre, ragged, scowling, wolfish, but prostrate, too, in their humility. Where graceful youth should have filled their features out, and touched them with its freshest tints, a stale and shrivelled hand, like that of age, had pinched and twisted them, and pulled them into shreds. Where angels might have sat enthroned, devils lurked, and glared out menacing. No change, no degradation, no perversion of humanity, in any grade, through all the mysteries of wonderful creation, has monsters half so horrible and dread.
>
> Scrooge started back, appalled. Having them shown to him in this way, he tried to say they were fine children, but the words choked themselves, rather than be parties to a lie of such enormous magnitude.[1]

The key here is the phrase "having them shown to him in this way." When the misery of people around you, "having been shown to you" through the eyes of God and their agony by the heart of

God, you are ready to dispense righteous judgment. Scrooge also felt the horror of his own hypocrisy—the plank in his own eye.

Today churches across America are committing a great crime against the Holy Spirit. Pastors have placed their opinion above the Word of God. Their priorities have filtered out the Holy Spirit. They have consulted marketeers the way King Saul consulted the witch of Endor (see 1 Sam. 28:7).

Jesus told us a central mission of the Holy Spirit: *"And when He has come, He will convict the world of sin, and of righteousness, and of judgment"* (John 16:8). Vital corrections and prophetic warnings of the Holy Spirit meant to save a nation were filtered out by a fabricated truce with sin.

In the process, they have created monsters—self-absorbed believers who are ignorant of the Bible, disarmed from combat, and useless in the crusade to bring America back to God.

Willian Lane Craig said: "Church historian and theologian David Wells had called our contemporary generation of pastors 'the new disablers' because they have abandoned the traditional role of the pastor as a broker of truth to his congregation and replaced it with a new managerial model drawn from the professional world which emphasizes leadership abilities, marketing, and administration. As a result the church has produced a generation of Christians for whom theology is irrelevant and whose lives outside the church do not differ practically from those of atheists."[2]

How else can you explain so-called believers voting for a party that hates God, Israel, marriage, and the unborn? How can they vote for their race or the promise of free stuff from the government instead of biblical morals?

Corban is a hideous example of what promoted Jesus to say, "Judge not." The Pharisees devised a way to appeal to greed by inventing Corban. Corban is a law whereby you can devote your wealth to God after you die but use it now.

This vile loophole was used to avoid the commandment to honor your mother and your father. A man could say to his parents, "The money I was using to help you is now Corban. I don't have to pay anymore because now it is devoted to God." This impoverished the elderly.

> *He answered and said to them, "Why do you also transgress the commandment of God because of your tradition? For God commanded, saying, 'Honor your father and your mother'; and, 'He who curses father or mother, let him be put to death.' But you say, 'Whoever says to his father or mother, "Whatever profit you might have received from me is a gift to God"—then he need not honor his father or mother.' Thus, you have made the commandment of God of no effect by your tradition"* (Matthew 15:3-6).

Corban got them out of a moral obligation of Jewish law.

How does that differ from pastors who today offer loopholes to get Christians out of their duties to holiness, revival, and witnessing? Remember when you hear them say "Jesus told me not to judge," they are doing the judging. *"Do not judge according to appearance, but judge with righteous judgment"* (John 7:24).

Now I want to show you the greatest danger of the end times. As my wife Mechelle and I walked on the National Mall in Washington D. C., we were overcome by the majesty, grandeur, and power of the United States. The iconic Washington Monument, Lincoln Memorial, and Capitol Building took our breath away. It all felt so powerful and permanent.

Suddenly, I was taken back to the time that the disciples walked among the capital buildings in Jerusalem that no doubt evoked the same kind of awe. As they were dumbfounded by the buildings, Jesus said, arguably, the most shocking thing He ever said to them:

Then Jesus went out and departed from the temple, and His disciples came up to show Him the buildings of the temple. And Jesus said to them, *"Do you not see all these things? Assuredly, I say to you, not one stone shall be left here upon another, that shall not be thrown down"* (Matthew 24:1-2).

This prediction rocked them to the core. It meant the destruction of the Jewish state. No way could these buildings be destroyed unless some army had first conquered the nation. In the same way, if these monuments of honor and power in Washington, D.C. were to be toppled until not one stone would be left upon another—it would mean that America is no more.

The disciples sheepishly ask for a timetable. "Now as He sat on the Mount of Olives, the disciples came to Him privately, saying, 'Tell us, when these things will be? And what will be the sign of Your coming, and of the end of the age?'" (Matthew 24:3).

Instead of giving them a date, He solemnly warns them of the greatest danger of the last days. What Jesus says must become the watchword for you in this chaotic time. *"And Jesus answered and said to them: 'Take heed that no one deceives you'"* (Matthew 24:4). Why is discernment at the top of Jesus' list of things to do to prepare for the last days? Shouldn't there be something else we do first? Shouldn't they have been instructed to store food and do fire drills and develop escape scenarios? Why discernment?

The answer is quite clear and simple. The chief danger in the last days is being deceived. Satan has saved his best lies for this moment—a moment when he can deceive the army of God into abandoning the front lines. How silly to believe that the devil would confuse the secular world so as to call evil good and good evil, yet not try the same thing within the Church. Hasn't the enemy tricked us into doing exactly what we should not be doing? We are reveling in doctrines of entitlement that make us flabby, indecisive, and easily offended—in a time that calls for humility, service, discipline and alertness.

This modern crime against the Holy Spirit has us believing things that are of God, are of the devil, and vice versa. Not judging righteously can mean you are refusing to see how God is working in your nation.

There are Christians who hate Trump. They suddenly developed a standard for presidents that no one ever had before. When you talk to them, they will tell you their newfound standard for voting—perfection. It's a standard that would have caused them to abstain from voting in every presidential election, all the way back to George Washington (because he was a Freemason).

The fact is that we must discern the purposes of God for Donald Trump.

Are you so set in your resentment that you can't see how clearly the battle lines are drawn?

Still don't know what you must do? From Nancy Pelosi to Alexandria Ocasio-Cortez, Democrats have vowed to open borders, seize guns, redistribute wealth, skyrocket taxes, and force the

Church to "evolve." The American Church still does not see the danger, and that itself is the danger.

These dumb ideas are not scriptural. They will play into the hands of those who would take away our rights and forever change America's system of government. It will be impossible to withstand the wave of falsehood and hatred in the next election if we do not repudiate these crippling dumb ideas.

But if we see them for what they are, rebuke them, and submit to the Holy Spirit, even a small number can create a mighty transformation.

Chapter 7

THE CRIME OF
FALSE SUBMISSION
TO GOVERNMENT

THE PERSON IN THE PULPIT SAYS, "WE WILL NOT LET politics into this church." Are they right? Maybe in some bubble of time in the 1950s. Today they are wrong. Back when we had civil discourse and bipartisan exchange of ideas, that statement might pass muster. But that day is gone. Why? Because the Left has turned politics into something new. They have made it a weapon for oppression. Their political policies are at war with Christianity.

The first duty of a pastor is to protect the sheep. An inner city pastor will speak out about such things as drug dealers and gang violence. Why? Because those hazards affect the daily lives of his congregation.

The pastor who refuses to clarify his political stand today is ignoring hazards his people face every day. Politics hurt. And you can't ignore the hurt it inflicts on your people.

Politics costs Christian bakers their business, gets believers fired in Far Left Silicon Valley; it can get one of your students expelled at school. Politics is why men in sexy women's clothes are reading to children in libraries. Politics is why you and I are accused of hate speech—speech that is simply the normal language of the Church. Politics is why many Christian outlets have stopped performing marriages. Politics is why your tax dollars fund the holocaust of abortion, which has laid a terrible curse on our land.

You did not leave the Democrat Party. They left you. They told the Church to get out. They openly booed God and Israel in their convention. They champion everything your Bible condemns. They are now controlled by the radical wing of their party—a wing that would gladly finance terror and give illegal criminals constitutional rights. What part of that is still unclear to you?

Staying out of politics is a recent trend for the Church. To hear some popular preachers, you'd think the Church was never led by God to be involved in politics. Not only has God used the Church in government—it is one of her chief roles in a society.

Charles Finney said, "No man can possibly be benevolent or religious, to the full extent of his obligations, without concerning himself, to a greater or less extent, with the affairs of human government."[1]

He also explained: "If there is a decay of conscience, the pulpit is responsible for it. If the public press lacks moral discernment, the pulpit is responsible for it. If the church is degenerate and worldly, the pulpit is responsible for it. If the world loses its interest in Christianity, the pulpit is responsible for it. If Satan rules in our halls of legislation, the pulpit is responsible for it. If our politics become so corrupt that the very foundations of our government are ready to fall away, the pulpit is responsible for it."[2]

From his death bed in 1791, John Wesley penned a note to William Wilberforce, a member of Parliament who had been converted under Wesley's ministry. Wilberforce was leading the charge to abolish slavery. This was the last letter Wesley wrote himself:

> Unless God has raised you up for this very thing, you will be worn out by the opposition of men and devils. But if God be for you, who can be against you? Are all of them together stronger than God? O be not weary of well doing! Go on, in the name of God and in the power of His might.[3]

It is hard to appreciate today how controversial it was to oppose slavery in that day. Many in the Church were caught up in an outrageous abuse of Scripture that gave them a "divine right" to own slaves. Even the liberals of that day looked the other way, thinking slaves were not truly worse off and the economic benefit outweighed the unsavory nature of slavery.

Liberal policies today enslave the poor by making them wholly dependent on social programs. The plantation is different, but the imperatives are the same. Then it was cash crops. Today they harvest votes.

Even Billy Graham, near the end of his life, felt compelled to buy space on billboards to instruct the Church to vote her conscience.

It's a high crime against the Holy Spirit not to guide the people on how to vote. It rips a weapon for good out of their hand. This is especially true when the battle lines are this clearly drawn.

But it is also essential that believers be reminded we are not an angry mob bent on creating a theocracy. We are acting against evil.

This is not about legislating morality; it's about stopping the legislation of immorality.

Now we move on to a burning question: Why did so many Christians vote to elect Barack Obama twice? Why did so many of them also vote for Hillary Clinton? The answer is not painless and strikes at the heart of this crime against the Holy Spirit. Many pastors refused to teach Bible doctrine.

When the Holy Spirit told leaders to teach doctrine—when the Spirit led them to search the Word and instill biblical morality in the people—they said no. They used the excuse that they didn't want to offend people.

So instead of creating an informed disciple and voter on the front end, they created a monster on the back end. And what's more offensive? The pastor who lays it out upfront and maybe loses a few in the audience, or the willful creation of a mutant with no convictions—a novice who can't discern good from evil or give an answer for their faith.

By the way, this sin is not relegated to seeker/attraction churches. Many Spirit-filled pastors also fell prey to not wanting to offend the fat cat tither who threatened to cut off funds "if you take certain stands."

Here are two bone-headed ideas:

1. All government is from God, and we must submit and not mention politics.

2. A candidate must be sinless before we can vote for them. Otherwise, we are choosing the lesser of two evils.

Here are the much-abused verses that are cited by those who commit these crimes:

> *Let every soul be subject to the governing authorities. For there is no authority except from God, and the authorities that exist are appointed by God. Therefore whoever resists the authority resists the ordinance of God, and those who resist will bring judgment on themselves. For rulers are not a terror to good works, but to evil. Do you want to be unafraid of the authority? Do what is good, and you will have praise from the same. For he is God's minister to you for good. But if you do evil, be afraid; for he does not bear the sword in vain; for he is God's minister, an avenger to execute wrath on him who practices evil* (Romans 13:1-4).

Do we stay out of politics and submit to government no matter what? No sane person believes Hitler was God's will for Germany. God brought down divine retribution upon the Nazis through the nations of the world. God works through people to restrain evil. The Church also has a duty to push back against evil.

"The authorities that exist" refers to authority endorsed by God, not rogue authority. Satan is rogue authority. That the Lord manipulates the devil does not mean He endorses the devil. God has always balanced the threat of tyranny with authorities He raises up: *"God's minister...to execute wrath on him who practices evil."*

Moreover, it tells us no ruling authority from God is a terror to good works. They do not persecute God's people or enact laws to ban the Gospel.

German believers abused these same verses to justify their apathy. Dietrich Bonhoeffer could not open the eyes of the German Church to the impending horrors of Hitler. His radio addresses warned Germany. Ironically, he blamed the fad of cheap grace and their blind submission. The point is that God works through people to stop evil. Bonhoeffer said, "Silence in the face of evil is itself evil, God will not hold us guiltless. Not to speak is to speak. Not to act is to act."[4] Pastors who stay out of the fight agree with the evil.

Nations can and do pick evil leaders. Even Israel picked an evil leader:

> *But the thing displeased Samuel when they said, "Give us a king to judge us." So Samuel prayed to the Lord. And the Lord said to Samuel, "Heed the voice of the people in all that they say to you; for they have not rejected you, but they have rejected Me, that I should not reign over them"* (1 Samuel 8:6-7).

Obama was never God's choice for America. We have a mountainous stockpile of moral wreckage to prove it.

When a minister says, "Everything is in God's hands, we need not do anything," they violate the way the Lord has chosen to work. He has limited Himself to answering prayer and moving hearts to be vessels. The comfort of knowing everything is in God's hands is wonderful, but it is not the message we need right now. We need to see that Heaven is not passive when evil reigns.

When evil reigns, God begins a complicated process to reestablish justice. Human history is messy. God works in that mess. We want fairy-tale endings, but humanity is complicated. Jehovah works like a surgeon skillfully cutting around vital organs to get at the cancer. Jesus spoke of the wheat and tares having to grow together until the end, otherwise the wheat would also be lost. We have a biblical mandate to discern and get involved in the work God is doing to save our nation.

This is why Peter violated a direct order from a rogue civil authority:

> *So they called them and commanded them not to speak at all nor teach in the name of Jesus. But Peter and John answered and said to them, "Whether it is right in the sight of God to listen to you more than to God, you judge. For we cannot but speak the things which we have seen and heard"* (Acts 4:18-20).

But the most important point to remember is that we did not pick this fight. They brought the fight to us. We didn't wander into politics; they invaded the Church. They jumped the fence into our yard. We did not spiritualize politics. They politicized spirituality. They wandered into our lane, ordering us to violate our conscience and worse—to disobey God.

Refusing to obey man's anti-God laws is not a violation of Romans 13; it is a confirmation of it. You cannot obey an evil law without disobeying a divine law. Remember Peter's injunction that we should obey God rather than man. Jesus said, *"No one can serve two masters"* (Matt. 6:24). Such obedience makes us an extension God's authority, not a rebel to it.

Another vivid picture of this is found in Acts chapter 16. Paul resisted a corrupt local government in Philippi. He acted for the welfare of the Church. A fresh body of believers faced its first attack from Satan, and Paul was not going to let evil go unchallenged.

But Paul said to them, They have beaten us openly, uncondemned Romans, and have thrown us into prison. And now do they put us out secretly? No indeed! Let them come themselves and get us out." And the officers told these words to the magistrates, and they were afraid when they heard that they were Romans. Then they came and pleaded with them and brought them out, and asked them to depart from the city. So they went out of the prison and entered the house of Lydia; and when they had seen the brethren, they encouraged them and departed (Acts 16:37-40).

Without this forceful resistance, the young Church would face severe future threats. Not only that, those fledgling Christians needed to see a model of the power of God. What Paul did is what many present leaders will not do. They did not present a unified voice for marriage or the holocaust of abortion—the worst savagery that has ever seen the light of day and has cursed our land. They offer only token resistance to evil legislation and abuse of power.

Now we turn to another fallacy of the modern Church and a crime against the Holy Spirit. It's loony to waste your right to vote because you "refuse to pick the lesser of two evils." You must discern where God is working and support it. God uses flawed people. No doubt, Daniel was shocked to see God using King Nebuchadnezzar.

Instead of seeking a sinless candidate, we should be asking where and through whom can God work.

Here's how Paul did it:

But when Paul perceived that the one part were Sadducees, and the other Pharisees, he cried out in the council, Men and brethren, I am a Pharisee, the son of a Pharisee: of the hope and resurrection of the dead I am called in question. And when he had so said, there arose a dissension between the Pharisees and the Sadducees: and the multitude was divided. For the Sadducees say that there is no resurrection, neither angel, nor spirit: but the Pharisees confess both. And there arose a great cry: and the scribes that were of the Pharisees' part arose, and strove, saying, we find no evil in this man: but if a spirit or an angel hath spoken to him, let us not fight against God (Acts 23:6-9).

Remember Jesus had exposed the error of both Sadducees and Pharisees. So was Paul choosing the lesser of two evils by siding with the Pharisees? Or, was he discerning where God could work? Right now, it's Trump He can work with. I just lost some of you.

Who can deny what happened on election night. Hillary Clinton was a shoo-in. She had the entire new media, Hollywood, all the tech giants of social media and twice the money that Trump had. CNN and MSNBC were drooling at the inevitability of a Clinton victory as they covered the unfolding drama. Then something strange began to unfold. One state after another began to fall to Trump. You could feel an unseen hand working its intention.

Trump is not the answer. He is a stay of execution to buy time for the Church to find her identity and destiny in the war that God is waging to save America.

These dumb ideas are not scriptural. They will play into the hands of those who would take away our rights and forever change America's system of government. It will be impossible to withstand the wave of falsehood and hatred in the next election if we do not repudiate these crippling, dumb ideas.

Even more urgent is the fact that we disobeyed the Holy Spirit's effort to push back on the evil that is such a menace now. It never should have come to this, but now that it has, it is time for deep repentance and a clear admission of the hurt done to the precious Spirit of God.

Without this clearing of our spirit, we cannot hope to be a part of the Godsend.

Chapter 8

THE CRIME OF ABUSING GRACE AND HOLINESS

I AM NOT INTERESTED IN NAMING NAMES TO EXPOSE THE falsehoods of hyper-grace teachers. No matter how much people salivate for me to mention names and zing their statements, I will stay on task. This is because the issue is not what a hyper-grace teacher said; it's about what people have become under their influence.

A sly teacher can couch their remarks to hide false doctrine. In a debate they can easily deflect criticism and camouflage their remarks by saying, "Here's what I meant." What they can't escape is the consistently garish behavior of people who practice what they teach. That's why Jesus said, *"By their fruits you shall know them"* (Matt. 7:16 DRA). In other words, what happens when people implement the teaching.

If there is nothing wrong with the hyper-grace message, why are so many drawing the same wrong conclusion? If it is not teaching a license to sin, why are so many using it as a license to sin? Why does this emphasis create an attitude of "how much of the world can I keep and still be right with God?" Why are so many turning this into a binge?

Our movement was once guilty of legalism. We used to judge people for their clothes, their makeup, and their hair length. We were guilty of seeing the outward appearance and not the heart. Those days are long gone. But the protest against them continues to create the opposite extreme. We just can't seem to strike a balance.

Satan despises balance with good reason. He understands that the right blend of joy and holiness, godliness with contentment, faith and love, and wisdom and boldness all produce powerful and lasting results. He must drive the Church to an extreme. He doesn't care which extreme it is.

Take revival for example. When it first appears, Satan will vehemently oppose it. When he sees that he can't stop it, he will run around behind it and push it to extremes.

In any imbalance, the key is to excite people over one single idea. In the fever of revelation they conclude that if a little is good then a lot is even better. You should be suspicious of any movement that always talks about the same thing. If you isolate a single truth to the exclusion of all others, you can turn it into a lie. This is why Martin Luther gave his pastors the requirement to preach every biblical doctrine within a year.

If all someone can talk about is grace, they are in trouble. But when they name their movement after it, they have fallen off the rails.

One of the best ways to understand grace is in these words from "Amazing Grace." It says, "Twas grace that taught my heart to fear, and grace my fears relieved."[1] To those in hyper-grace I must ask, "Did grace teach your heart to fear God?" To those who oppose grace I will ask, "Did grace relieve your fears?"

But how is this grace abuse a crime against the Holy Spirit? Not only is it a crime, it is one of the most dangerous of all the crimes I will talk about. This teaching on grace has an impact on much more that we think. Not only does it impact those who heartily embrace it, it has touched virtually every aspect of church life.

Even those who don't agree with hyper-grace still behave in a manner that is far too casual about the holy things of God. The collateral damage of cheapened grace is why we have coarse language in the pulpit, scantily clad worship leaders, and leaders who get drunk and are hooked on pornography. The looseness from hyper-grace has released a shallowness toward prayer, soul-winning, and discipleship in general. It is why so many church gatherings are not just casual but crude. It's why you often cringe at the shenanigans that pass for a worship service.

A stupor has settled over the people of God that blurs the lines of what is sacred and secular—what is urgent and what is nonchalant—leaving us with people who are not hungry, burdened, or even curious about seeking the Holy Spirit.

Some have even turned grace into a weapon against authority. It is not a coincidence that many who have glommed on to cheap grace have left their church. At first, they claim it is to find a new family of believers who agree with their new insight on God. But I have noticed they often end up out of church completely, bringing their self-centered ways to their logical conclusion.

Grace is cheapened by Satan for good reason. Few things handicap a child of God faster than the lie that grace is an inexhaustible source of credit to do whatever you want. Bonhoeffer said, "Grace is represented as the Church's inexhaustible treasury, from which she showers blessings with generous hands, without asking questions or fixing limits. Grace without price; grace without cost! The essence of grace, we suppose, is that the account has been paid in advance; and, because it has been paid, everything can be had for nothing. Since the cost was infinite, the possibilities of using and spending it are infinite."[2]

No wonder Paul issued a warning to Timothy that is even more glaring when you consider today's contaminated crowd. *"But you be watchful in all things, endure afflictions, do the work of an evangelist, fulfill your ministry"* (2 Tim. 4:5).

"But you" infers that many will be compelled to satisfy the aberrant appetites of the contaminated audience. He's saying, "A lot of teachers are going to be sucked into this, but you stand your ground and hold your integrity."

"Endure afflictions" means that you may be shocked to see that the most painful disappointments may not come from the world at all, but from a church that oppresses you for preaching the truth.

"Do the work of an evangelist"—just because they, in their gluttonous selfishness, no longer care about lost souls, you keep reaching the lost.

This cheapened-grace virus is a high crime against the Holy Spirit. It is one big reason the army of God didn't notice the gathering darkness over America. Even if they did, they were too groggy and flabby to respond to the Holy Spirit's urgings to get ready. Which leads to the final fruit of this hideous tendency.

Under the spell of the contaminated crowd, preachers find themselves attacking people who want to be holy. How dare you punish a heart for wanting purity? How can it be that vessels chosen to uplift the righteous and equip the saints instead accuse hungry hearts of having a religious spirit?

They reserve their praise for those aren't even trying to serve God. Honestly, does it look like the Church is wearing herself out to serve and follow Jesus? You'd sure think so by the way some ministers keep telling the people to relax and quit trying so hard, because Daddy is so pleased with them.

Even when a congregation is a listless, flabby, biblically illiterate, club of moody consumers, preachers will pamper them with one more high-calorie pep talk about how much God is pleased with them. It has gotten so bad that Sundays are a celebration of how much God lets you get away with.

They seem so easygoing. And why wouldn't they be, after all the soothing guarantees of God's unconditional approval. But don't be fooled. All that veneer of serenity explodes when they come into contact with holiness. That's why they must attack it on sight.

Gently suggest the Church could go deeper, call for more prayer meetings, voice concern about inappropriate behavior, tell them you don't want to party with them, and they will scream, *"You have a religious spirit!"*

What was once normal discipleship, is now legalistic. Anything that dampens their festivities is judgmental.

What have we done? We have unleashed a counterfeit liberty. These are not the features of a Spirit-led people. These are the symptoms of a people with sick souls deceived and careening toward disaster.

Here is a chilling Scripture that speaks to the evil that is twisting the Church. Isaiah 59:15 says: *"So truth fails, and he who departs from evil makes himself a prey. Then the Lord saw it, and it displeased Him that there was no justice."*

The greatest gift God can send a church is a holy child of God. Their heart is toward revival. They want the fire, glory, and power of God to electrify the church. Make them your enemy and you have also made an enemy out of God. The grace of God would never do this.

Again, Bonhoeffer concludes: "Cheap grace is the preaching of forgiveness without requiring repentance, baptism without church discipline, Communion without confession, absolution without personal confession. Cheap grace is grace without discipleship, grace without the cross, grace without Jesus Christ, living and incarnate."[3]

Cheap grace is a modern crime against the Holy Spirit.

Chapter 9

THE CRIME OF THE CONTAMINATED CROWD

ARRY HOUDINI IS ONE OF THE MOST FAMOUS ESCAPE artists in history. There was only one trap he couldn't escape: his audience.

His demise began on October 11, 1926.[1] While being shackled into his Chinese Water Torture Cell during a performance in Albany, New York, Harry Houdini was struck by a piece of faulty equipment and broke his left ankle.

His doctor told him to cancel his tour. Instead the magician carried on to Montreal. While there, he gave a lecture at McGill University. On October 22 he invited some McGill students to visit him in his dressing room at the Princess Theater.

A student named J. Gordon Whitehead asked Houdini if it was true that he could take hard punches to his stomach. Houdini said the rumors were true. Without warning, Whitehead delivered forceful and well-aimed punches to his stomach. Houdini was not ready for the punches as he was plopped down on a couch due to his ankle pain.

This is where the story gets tricky. Houdini dismissed the pain from those punches and did the show that night. His pain only got worse when he took a train to Detroit for his next engagement.

Soon he had severe pain, cold sweats, fatigue, and a fever of 104 degrees. A doctor suspected appendicitis and told him to go to a hospital. Instead, the conjurer went on with the show and collapsed right after the final curtain. It would be his last show.

That night doctors removed his appendix. They found that it had burst days before. Houdini's death was listed as peritonitis caused by a ruptured appendix. At the time, they thought the blows to his abdomen burst his appendix. Today we know that is extremely unlikely. But those punches did mask the real threat—a threat, that if known in time, could have saved his life.

Houdini's audience wanted more. The pressure to present a more dazzling escape ultimately took his life. Even when he didn't want to perform—even when he wasn't on a stage—the audience never let him off the hook. He couldn't resist the need to please them.

Now read the following verses with a view to Houdini's obsession:

> *I charge you therefore before God and the Lord Jesus Christ, who will judge the living and the dead at His appearing and His kingdom: Preach the word! Be ready in season and out of season. Convince, rebuke, exhort, with all longsuffering and teaching. For the time will come when they will not endure sound doctrine, but according to their own desires, because they have itching ears, they will heap up for themselves teachers; and they will turn their ears away from the*

truth, and be turned aside to fables. But you be watch-
ful in all things, endure afflictions, do the work of an
evangelist, fulfill your ministry (2 Timothy 4:1-5).

I realize these verses are a favorite of preachers who are angry or jealous of anything new that God does in His people. Nevertheless, it is a solemn warning. It is the last words of a father to his son in the Lord. However, the real warning in these verses is constantly overlooked.

If you think these verses warn against false teachers, look closer. You will see the following pronouns in order: *they, their, they, they, themselves, they,* and *their.* The false teacher is mentioned only once. The audience is mentioned seven times! This is not a warning to the people about preachers. This is a warning to a preacher about the audience.

Paul is warning his spiritual son about being thrown off course by the wanton appetites of the crowd. After reading about the magician, you can see why I call this pitfall the Houdini syndrome. In the previous chapter I mentioned the contaminated crowd, let me develop the subject.

Even reputable ministries are subject to the Houdini syndrome. I have watched dear friends drift from solid content to wild fantasies. The audience resonates with something they said. The speaker (allow me to misuse an adjective to create a new verb) profounds the audience. Swooning behind the depth of the preacher's remark, the people pull for more.

The speaker feels adulation and wanders beyond their original teaching, beyond what God told them to preach. Soon they are having an out-of-Bible experience.

For too long we have placed the focus on the error of false ministries without addressing the scourge that keeps them going. It's like the argument about the flow of drugs into our nation. We focus on the cartels but ignore that fact that it is the users buying the drugs who keep them in business. Until we do something about demand, we will never stop the supply. For every fraudulent preacher, there is a consumer. For every zany prophet, a zany groupie.

But the problem is wider than this. Again, borrowing from the war on drugs, the problem is not just suppliers and users, it is the permissive society. When you glorify pleasure and remove the shame, you enable addiction. Our culture even rewards people for giving into baser drives.

Pulpit subject matter today is largely derived from what the crowd wants to hear. Once a topic sells, they run it into the ground. Every book will be about the buzzword. Every new worship song will feature it. Every sermon will give a new slant on the revelation du jour.

When it comes to drawing a crowd, discernment seems to go out the window. If a pop star whose music is blatantly immoral can pack a church, preachers will invite them.

To say that the Spirit-filled Church has grown permissive is an understatement. Instead of catalyzing change, we are sponging in the culture. The sharp edge of discernment has been dulled by an influx of congregants who influence pastors through flattery and seduction.

The teacher with the itching ear has uncoupled from the Holy Spirit and is overly connected to their audience. Some traveling ministries scour the internet and social media to get the buzzwords of today. You see them claiming to have dreams and visions with greater and greater frequency. They know how people clamor to hear about exotic experiences. Remember, this hankering to hear about dreams and visions has its root in impatience: *"They will not endure sound doctrine."* The bottom line is, they are looking for a shortcut.

Notice how when the disciples asked Jesus about the last days, the first thing He mentioned was deception. Matthew 24:4 says, *"And Jesus answered and said to them: 'Take heed that no one deceives you.'"* The Greek word for deceive in this verse is *planáō*. According to Strong's concordance it means "to (properly, cause to) roam (from safety, truth, or virtue):—go astray, deceive, err, seduce, wander, be out of the way."[2]

Planáō is where we get the word planet.[3] Planets are in an orbit. A subtle deviation of Earth's orbit—by even just a few degrees—would soon cause a catastrophe. *Planáō* can also be said to mean being thrown out of orbit. The Houdini effect on a preacher is also subtle. It begins undetected but soon grows to full-blown deception.

You can see this disastrous trajectory in verse 4: *"And they will turn their ears away from the truth, and be turned aside to fables."* We see this today. Ministries that once offered solid content, add titillating tidbits here and there until finally, they are flat-out making things up.

In a frenzy to stay popular some will steal the revelation of other preachers and claim them as their own. Jeremiah 23:30 says, *"'Therefore behold, I am against the prophets,' says the Lord, 'who steal My words every one from his neighbor.'"*

You don't tune a piano to another piano. You use tuning forks. Likewise, nothing matters more to a servant of God than their private walk with Jesus. Nothing else will have the ring of truth.

Isaiah 50:4 describes this tuning process perfectly: *"The Lord God has given Me the tongue of the learned, that I should know how to speak a word in season to him who is weary. He awakens Me morning by morning, He awakens My ear to hear as the learned."*

This modern crime against the Holy Spirit has done vast damage. Like all the others in this section, this one has weakened and divided the army of God at a critical moment in America's life. Satan used this to make sure we were neutralized while he was destroying America's life. He tricked us into gathering fans instead of releasing disciples.

Now witness an outstanding example of a prophet who overcame the tractor pull of the contaminated crowd. That prophet is Micaiah, one of four men trained under Elijah.

In First Kings 22, Ahab, king of Israel, wants to talk Jehoshaphat, king of Judah, into joining him in battle to win back Ramoth Gilead from Syria. Though willing, Jehoshaphat wants to be sure God is in this venture.

Ahab summons four hundred prophets. They all say that victory is assured. Jehoshaphat is bothered by the mass agreement and asks if there is one more prophet. Ahab's response says it all: *"There is still one man, Micaiah the son of Imlah, by whom we may inquire of the Lord; but I hate him, because he does not prophesy good concerning me, but evil"* (1 Kings 22:8).

Here is the contaminated crowd that will only listen to positive prophecies.

They send a man to go get Micaiah. What this messenger says to the prophet is like holding up a mirror to the modern Spirit-filled Church: *"Then the messenger who had gone to call Micaiah spoke to him, saying, 'Now listen, the words of the prophets with one accord encourage the king. Please, let your word be like the word of one of them, and speak encouragement'"* (1 Kings 22:13).

How often have pastors overruled the Holy Spirit by insisting the guest speaker say only positive things to the audience?

Now witness the man of God giving the proper response to this indecent request: *"And Micaiah said, 'As the Lord lives, whatever the Lord says to me, that I will speak'"* (1 Kings 22:14).

Now we come to one of the greatest moments of courage in history. Micaiah walks into a scene of crushing intimidation. Two kings wearing royal robes sit on thrones staring down at him. One has murder in his eyes. Around him are four hundred false prophets who have all given the exact same "word from the Lord." A vast crowd overflows the royal hall. A dead silence falls when Ahab orders the prophet to prophesy.

Think about it. Micaiah tells Ahab he will be killed in the battle for Ramoth Gilead. It goes even deeper. He reveals to Ahab that a lying spirit has put lies in the mouth of all the prophets. This is the judgement of God—to fool Ahab to go to his death.

This deception is so deep that even telling Ahab about it will not stop him. Micaiah says in verse 23: *"Therefore look! The Lord has put a lying spirit in the mouth of all these prophets of yours, and the Lord has declared disaster against you."* Ahab is seduced by his audience of prophets. He goes to war. A random arrow finds a kink in his armor. He dies right on schedule.

Unlike Houdini, Jesus tried to get away from crowds. He loved them but didn't care about what they wanted to hear. He only spoke what the Father gave Him. The Holy Spirit carries on that great mandate.

Second Timothy 2:15 says, *"Be diligent to present yourself approved to God, a worker who does not need to be ashamed, rightly dividing the word of truth." Rightly dividing* means several things. One thing it means is that you don't beat one subject to death. Another thing it means is that you filter out your private opinion. Your message must also be free of flattery and compliance to group think.

Billy Graham spent as much time discerning what not to say as much as what to say. He wanted to speak the words that had the Holy Spirit's approval. He knew those words might come off sounding simple, but it didn't matter because he knew God would empower them.

Seek the approval of God, not audiences. If you obey God, the crowds, as Billy Graham discovered, will come anyway. Only this time their appetite will be for truth, and you will advance the Kingdom of God and not a counterfeit. We must repent of grieving the Holy Spirit by catering to the contaminated crowd.

Matthew Henry said, "Wise and good men, though they covet to do good, yet are far from coveting to have it talked of when it is done; because it is God's acceptance, not men's applause, that they aim at."[4]

A contaminated audience will shower you with money and fame if you keep the rightful demands of God off their backs. They will also lead you to disaster. Just because a message is popular does not make it truth. It has been said that a speaker should know his audience. I say they should know what God wants them to say to that audience.

A friend of mine was stunned and frightened when he heard a famous hyper-grace teacher say, "I must be right; look at all the people who are following me."

Chapter 10

THE CRIME OF WITHHOLDING THE BAPTISM IN THE HOLY SPIRIT

NOTHING CONTRIBUTED MORE TO THE SLIDE INTO irrelevance of the Spirit-filled/Charismatic/ Pentecostal movement than the crime we are about to examine. This is why it was saved for last in this section.

We begin with a simple question: Whatever happened to the baptism in the Holy Spirit? You don't hear about it anymore. Churches don't pray with people to receive it anymore. There's an ugly reason why.

The baptism of the Holy Spirit is the natural enemy of church marketing that seeks not to offend. When God falls, church culture changes instantly. Human promotion becomes secondary. An audience morphs into an army. An insatiable hunger for the Word of God reduces the need for sales pitches.

Preacher, if you stopped presenting the baptism of the Holy Spirit to your people, Satan made you do it. If there is no room in your service for people to receive this urgent gift, the enemy seized control of your agenda. If your people don't even know what it is, you will answer to God.

No matter how noble, persuasive, or convincing the argument, the decision to exclude the baptism of the Holy Spirit from the life of the Church, is a decision conceived in hell.

This gift is so urgent, the Church was forbidden to begin operations until they had received it. Acts 1:4-5 says:

> *And being assembled together with them, He commanded them not to depart from Jerusalem, but to wait for the Promise of the Father, "which," He said, "you have heard from Me; for John truly baptized with water, but you shall be baptized with the Holy Spirit not many days from now."*

The apostles deemed it so essential that they immediately prescribe it to any believer who has not received it.

> *Now when the apostles who were at Jerusalem heard that Samaria had received the word of God, they sent Peter and John to them, who, when they had come down, prayed for them that they might receive the Holy Spirit"* (Acts 8:14-15).
>
> *And it happened, while Apollos was at Corinth, that Paul, having passed through the upper regions, came to Ephesus. And finding some disciples he said to them, "Did you receive the Holy Spirit when you believed?" So they said to him, "We have not so much as heard whether there is a Holy Spirit." And he said to them, "Into what then were you baptized?" So they*

said, *"Into John's baptism." Then Paul said, "John indeed baptized with a baptism of repentance, saying to the people that they should believe on Him who would come after him, that is, on Christ Jesus." When they heard this, they were baptized in the name of the Lord Jesus. And when Paul had laid hands on them, the Holy Spirit came upon them, and they spoke with tongues and prophesied* (Acts 19:1-6).

This is the condition Paul was warning us of in Second Timothy 3:5: *"Having a form of godliness, but denying the power thereof"* (KJV). It created an entire generation living out their faith by their own power.

And why are we currently swimming in false teaching, false prophecy, and false Christianity? Excluding the baptism in the Holy Spirit opened the door to widespread heresy. All across the internet, ministries dabble in New Age hybrids of Christian faith, exotic extremes, drunkenness, and even perversion.

Noted Christian apologist Ravi Zacharias said, "I had dinner with a preacher [with a Spirit-filled background] who claims he speaks to more people via television than anyone else in the world. He told me there is not much difference between Islam and Christianity."

Where can we hang the blame for that and all the other foolishness but on the lack of the indwelling power of the Holy Spirit? Neglecting the baptism of the Holy Spirit did this. Why? Because the Holy Spirit is not just a power experience; He is the Spirit of truth.

Jesus said, *"However, when He, the Spirit of truth, has come, He will guide you into all truth; for He will not speak on His own authority, but whatever He hears He will speak; and He will tell you things to come"* (John 16:13).

If Jesus calls the Holy Spirit the Spirit of truth, what happens to truth without Him? It is by His leading, His power, and His presence that we first discern truth from error. There is a Spirit of truth and there is a spirit of error. You know the difference by the indwelling Holy Spirit.

The absence of the baptism is why we have two extremes. We have those who believe nothing and those who believe everything. Both are products of a lack of discernment and power. It is only after you experience the real presence and power of God that you truly hunger for the Bible and know what is fake from what is real.

Look at the discipleship attitude result of the baptism of the Holy Spirit on the day of Pentecost:

> *Then those who gladly received his word were baptized; and that day about three thousand souls were added to them. And they continued steadfastly in the apostles' doctrine and fellowship, in the breaking of bread, and in prayers. Then fear came upon every soul, and many wonders and signs were done through the apostles* (Acts 2:41-43).

The next verse reveals the most devastating result of banning the baptism in the Holy Spirit.

> *But you shall receive power when the Holy Spirit has come upon you; and you shall be witnesses to Me in Jerusalem, and in all Judea and Samaria, and to the end of the earth* (Acts 1:8).

Soul winning is always the first thing Satan removes from church life. Not only does the baptism in the Holy Spirit add soul winning, it also makes the witness itself vibrant, compelling, and contagious. For a very good reason.

Jesus did not say, "You shall do witnessing." He said, "You shall be witnesses." The baptism creates soul winners. Sharing their faith is not an act for them; it is their natural being. Because they are a witness, they continually express the Gospel—even when they are not aware of it.

There are a great many programs to instruct believers on how to share their faith. But the worldwide explosion of the Pentecostal movement cannot be traced back to any such training.

Spirit-baptized believers do not mechanically, apologetically, or stodgily dispense their faith—they spill it. It emanates from them. As a matter of fact, most are not smooth at giving a witness. Often they violate basic laws of persuasion but more than compensate for it with radiant joy and disarming sincerity. Outsiders do not so much hear a sermon put feel it. The Spirit-filled witness carries an atmosphere with them.

Because we have now peopled the pews with many who are not converted, we are dubious to tell them about the baptism in the Holy Spirit. That does brutal damage to the Church. We gain numbers but lose ground. Charles Spurgeon said, "To introduce unconverted persons to the church, is to weaken and degrade it; and therefore an apparent gain may be a real loss."[1]

The preacher who consciously withholds the baptism in the Holy Spirit is a traitor. They are aiding and abetting the enemy. They are withholding a priceless gift bought and paid for by the blood of Jesus. They keep from the children of God an edge of power that would make the believer strong, alert, and able to win others. The baptism endows them with a priceless tool, a prayer language, that pierces all adversity. How dare we hold this back!

The Pentecostal revival is the greatest Christian revival in history. Beginning in the humble Azusa Street Mission, it has blazed on for more than one hundred years, with more than seven hundred million converts. Only one thing explains it: the baptism in the Holy Spirit.

SECTION III

Introduction

EMBRACING THE GODSEND

THE HOLY SPIRIT IS AMASSING AN ARMY. THE FIRST signs are frustration and agitation. Praying people will feel out of sorts. They don't fit into church incorporated. Their turmoil will lead to an experience in the glory of God.

It begins with a renewed relationship with the Holy Spirit and greater intimacy with Christ. You will advance to an understanding of flowing in true signs and wonders and not the sad emotional imitations.

From there you will find your assignment in God's war to save America. Your task will overtake you with blazing clarity. It will be a mission that commands all of your talents. It is an endeavor you can easily see yourself doing for the rest of your life.

July 8th, 2021

103

Chapter 11

SEPARATE TO ME

THE HOLY SPIRIT IS SEPARATING A SELECT GROUP TO Himself. He means to imbue them with special grace and power to accomplish mighty acts at the edge of history. They will be uniquely equipped to face the sophisticated evil of our time. But it all begins by making peace with the Holy Spirit and restoring Him to His rightful place.

Take a close look at the Book of Acts, and you will see the disarming, down-to-earth way that they related to the Holy Spirit. While they revered Him deeply, they had a sense of His nearness and His involvement in their day-to-day operations. They behaved as if He was close by and they could almost see Him. Most of all, they anticipated His instructions.

> As they ministered to the Lord and fasted, the Holy Spirit said, "Now separate to Me Barnabas and Saul for the work to which I have called them." Then, having fasted and prayed, and laid hands on them, they sent them away. So, being sent out by the Holy Spirit, they went down to Seleucia, and from there they sailed to Cyprus (Acts 13:2-4).

What did that look like? All we get from Luke is that they knew the Holy Spirit had spoken. We get no indication of any method they used to confirm divine instructions. It's a good thing too. Our carnal nature always looks for shortcuts. What we do know is that they fasted, worshipped, and prayed.

Not only did they know when to go, they also knew when to stop.

> *Now when they had gone through Phrygia and the region of Galatia, they were forbidden by the Holy Spirit to preach the word in Asia. After they had come to Mysia, they tried to go into Bithynia, but the Spirit did not permit them* (Acts 16:6-7).

We cannot calculate the devastating cost we have paid for building churches and ministries by our own wits. We seem to gauge our service to God by activity. But if we only went out at the bidding of the Holy Spirit, we would see astounding results.

Their secret is this: they obeyed the original instructions Jesus left them about how to surrender to the Holy Spirit. If we have any hope of having the power we need in this hour, we must revisit the moment Jesus began to introduce the disciples to this wondrous person. We need a fresh look at what Jesus said about why the Spirit would come, how much power He would have, and what His mandate was.

In a way, this is a fearful reckoning. The ground you are about to cover is so sacred that each step will expose the deepest intents of your heart. Hidden motives will surface. The person seeking personal glory or an edge to success should proceed no further.

Remember the sorcerer who tried to buy the imparting the Holy Spirit? Peter told him, *"Your money perish with you, because you thought that the gift of God could be purchased with money! You have neither part nor portion in this matter, for your heart is not right in the sight of God"* (Acts 8:20-21).

The paradox of the Holy Spirit is this: while He urgently seeks vessels to use, He is equally willing to walk away and find someone else if we play games with Him.

When Jesus explained the coming of the Holy Spirit, He began with news that shocked the disciples: *"I am going away"* (John 8:21).

Try to fathom the impact that news had on them. The tide of public opinion had turned against them. It was an explosively volatile situation. They were still so untrained for the task before them. They must have felt a crushing sense of abandonment.

This is where the Church stumbles. We take away a wholly inadequate understanding. The Spirit of God is not a consolation prize. He was not sent to merely fill the vacuum Jesus left behind. They were not just breaking even. Jesus said it was to their advantage that He leave. And what an advantage!

> *But because I have said these things to you, sorrow has filled your heart. Nevertheless I tell you the truth. It is to your advantage that I go away; for if I do not go away, the Helper will not come to you; but if I depart, I will send Him to you. And when He has come, He will convict the world of sin, and of righteousness, and of judgment: of sin, because they do not believe in Me; of righteousness, because I go to My Father and you*

see Me no more; of judgment, because the ruler of this world is judged. I still have many things to say to you, but you cannot bear them now. However, when He, the Spirit of truth, has come, He will guide you into all truth; for He will not speak on His own author- ity, but whatever He hears He will speak; and He will tell you things to come. He will glorify Me, for He will take of what is Mine and declare it to you. All things that the Father has are Mine. Therefore I said that He will take of Mine and declare it to you (John 16:6-15).

Let's look at the advantages: Jesus had come in bodily form. He operated from one physical location at a time. Now He had finished that phase of His mission. The power would increase exponentially. The Holy Spirit is not limited to one location; He is omnipresent. He would fall on all flesh.

In one moment, on the day of Pentecost, the Church stopped being a ragtag prayer huddle in an obscure upper room. Suddenly from Heaven, they became a global force supervised by an invisible person who was at once enveloping the world with conviction and serving as commander in chief of the armed forces of the Body of Christ on Earth. And doing it with all the power God the Father had given to Jesus.

Let's rehearse the implication. All the power to, as Paul said, "tear down strongholds." All the wisdom ever needed to decode cultures, avoid traps, speak with a mouth that Jesus promised *"your adversaries shall not be able to gainsay nor resist"* (Luke 21:15 KJV). I could go on and on.

The Holy Spirit was never meant as a supplement we add to our ideas and talents. He is not the mysterious force we reluctantly go to in emergencies. He is not the final option; He is the only option.

I would go so far as to say that no matter how noble our endeavor—no matter how pure and worthy it seems—they actually aid the enemy if they were not born of the Holy Spirit. Maybe now you can understand why I was so adamant in the section about modern crimes against the Holy Spirit.

All our failures, in all the battles—all the ground the enemy has taken—all the morals and freedoms we have lost in America can be traced back to our activity outside the Holy Spirit.

But John 16:15 must be restated: *"All things that the Father has are Mine. Therefore I said that He will take of Mine and declare it to you."* Here is an astounding fact: the Spirit wants to declare to us everything that Jesus has. This *purpose* of the Holy Spirit is reinforced by Paul the Apostle: *"Now we have received, not the spirit of the world, but the Spirit who is from God, that we might know the things that have been freely given to us by God"* (1 Cor. 2:12).

All the glittering fool's gold and false success of Christian empires can only be exposed if God reveals to us what we might have had if we had obeyed the Holy Spirit. But is it not too late. God is warring yet again to marshal a great force of change in America.

This also brings us to the great hope of this book: God is separating to Himself a core who can have the precise relationship with the Holy Spirit that they had in the Book of Acts. Look at those words again "separate to Me." This was not just a call to be set apart but also to come nearer to the Holy Spirit.

Relearning dependency of the Holy Spirit and leaving mindless activity is not easy. And even the best of us have been fooled. Listen to what David Wilkerson said, "I knew the blessing was not in building. Not in some well-planned scheme to reach the lost. Not in bigness, and not in activity. I discovered the hard way, that the glory of God, the peace and joy of the Spirit, was in being stripped down, emptied, and made totally weak. God had to expose all my values. He turned His flaming eyes on my soul and showed me I had better reject my old way of doing things, or be lost in a maze of self-imposed activity."[1]

Look around you. You see the great falling away. You see that even many who remained in church are mired in systems that are lifeless and compromised. On the other hand, you see a core comparing notes, saying, "There has to be more. This flashy, showy version can't be right." They are praying. They are hungering. They are being separated from the contaminated crowd.

This separation by the Spirit was predicted by Smith Wigglesworth:

> We have to see that these days have to come before the Lord can come. There has to be a falling away.... I want to speak to you very exactly. All the people who are pressing into and getting ready for this glorious, attained place where they will not be found naked, where they will be blameless, where they will be immovable, where they will be purified by the power of the Word of God, have within them a consciousness of the very presence of God. They know that God is working in them, changing their very nature and preparing

them for a greater thing and causing them to be ready for translation....

This is the day of purifying; this is the day of holiness; this is the day of separation; this is the day of waking. Oh, God, let us wake today! Let our inner spirits wake into consciousness that God is calling us....

There are in the world two classes of believers. There are believers who are disobedient—or I ought to say there are children who are saved by the power of God, but who are disobedient children—and there are children who are also saved by the power of God who are longing to be more obedient all the time.[2]

Wilkerson talked about a "work" within us. Wigglesworth talked about "pressing in." The image is clear: the Holy Spirit is stirring souls across the nation. They are done with the overuse of big screens, skinny jeans, and fog machines. They are being pulled away from fleshly things even as a spirit of prayer is overtaking them. They are surrendering to a special work of the Holy Spirit.

Paul described this dividing apart and pulling away. He even gave the formula for satisfying this deep hunger for more:

> *But in a great house there are not only vessels of gold and silver, but also of wood and clay, some for honor and some for dishonor. Therefore if anyone cleanses himself from the latter, he will be a vessel for honor, sanctified and useful for the Master, prepared for every good work* (2 Timothy 2:20-21).

How do we surrender to the Holy Spirit? How do we honor His invitation to be separated unto Him?

Amazingly, the best answer may be found in the Old Testament—a treasure in simple verses we have read many times. Look at them now with fresh eyes. *"Trust in the Lord with all your heart, and lean not on your own understanding; in all your ways acknowledge Him, and He shall direct your paths"* (Prov. 3:5-6). How can these simple words help in such a deep situation?

It is wrapped up in four words: *trust, lean not,* and *acknowledge.*

Trust. All ambition to succeed can only be abandoned with trust. You must believe that if your heart will concern itself with the matters of the Kingdom of God, the Holy Spirit will concern Himself with the matters of your heart.

You can only finally let go and trust when you believe God sees the desires of your heart. Dying to our dreams and goals to follow the Spirit's leading, places those dreams and goals in the safest possible hands. Psalm 37:4 says, *"Delight yourself also in the Lord, and He shall give you the desires of your heart."* But no one said it better than Jesus: *"But seek first the kingdom of God and His righteousness, and all these things shall be added to you"* (Matt. 6:33).

Lean not to your own understanding. Don't get me wrong. God does not want us passive. He wants us aggressive in action. Remember that even when the Holy Spirit stopped Paul twice in Acts 16, it meant that Paul was trying to go somewhere. It is simply that the Spirit of God wants our action to be directed. Even waiting on God is active. It must expect wisdom and be conscious of the rewards of obedience.

James 1:5 says, *"If any of you lacks wisdom, let him ask of God, who gives to all liberally and without reproach, and it will be given to him."* Hebrews 11:6 tells us, *"But without faith it is impossible to please Him, for he who comes to God must believe that He is, and that He is a rewarder of those who diligently seek Him."*

Acknowledge Him in all your ways. Nothing is so important as this last truth. Remember how we began with the practical way the disciples engaged the Holy Spirit in all their ways? Let me explain how this works. It does not mean we become robots that can't think or act for ourselves. It is a question of honor.

Say you are visiting a friend. You are in the kitchen and you want a glass of milk. You know they will say yes if you ask, but you would feel odd just walking over to their refrigerator and helping yourself. This is a case of honoring them—acknowledging it is their house.

It is ridiculous to think we are to go through a day waiting for guidance for every move we make. We can however walk effortlessly through our day honoring the Holy Spirit's impulse and influence on our choices.

Let me finish with a story that illustrates how easily we exclude the Holy Spirit. Before I was to go out and preach, I was with a pastor in his office. He mentioned another preacher who had been there a few months before. He said, "He will never preach in my church again."

I immediately rebuked him. I said, "You are wrong if you didn't first go to that brother and help him understand what he did wrong. Secondly, you are wrong because you said, 'my church.' It is not your church, and you do not have the final say who preaches here and who does not. That authority belongs to the Holy Spirit."

We wonder why we lack power and miracles. We wonder why we have lost so much in so short a time in America. Beloved, are you being separated to Him? Then surrender in complete joy at the honor of being selected to walk with the Holy Spirit in end-time power and wisdom.

Chapter 12

YOUR ASSIGNMENT IN THE GODSEND

GOD IS WARRING TO SAVE AMERICA. YOU MUST FIND your assignment in that war. But how can we know our assignment? Think about it. It is fashionable to teach that the will of God is hard to know. But does that make any sense? We quote these verses:

> *I beseech you therefore, brethren, by the mercies of God, that you present your bodies a living sacrifice, holy, acceptable to God, which is your reasonable service. And do not be conformed to this world, but be transformed by the renewing of your mind, that you may prove what is that good and acceptable and perfect will of God (Romans 12:1-2).*

We think we see a torturous process in these Scriptures. But look again. It says, "reasonable service." Nothing these verses demand go beyond what every Christian is supposed to do anyway. This signifies something critical. It means the will of God is utterly knowable. You want to know, and God wants to show it.

The great skill of the Holy Spirit is to make you able to know and do the will of God. Again, this is your reasonable service. It is all the added human speculation that makes it complicated.

Speaking of complicated, nothing has muddied the waters more than a bad takeaway from the concept of "a purpose-driven life." This is no slap at Rick Warren or his book. This is about the abuse of his book.

Many have taken it to mean they should pursue an independent course. They ooze with, "I gotta be me." They think, "God's purpose is what makes me unique, so I will pursue uniqueness." Values get blurred, and they become self-centered. Soon sacrifice, obedience, and service don't fit into their "purpose."

Imagine a young recruit in the Marines. The first day of boot camp he is standing at attention and his drill instructor barks a question at him: "Why did you join the Marine Corps?"

Imagine the young grunt answering, "To find my purpose." About three days later, when the swelling in his eyes and the ringing in his ears subside, he can hear the sergeant screaming, "You have no purpose! Only the corps has a purpose! What you have is an assignment!"

Let me break it to you gently. A better word than *purpose* is *assignment*. Aren't we to be purpose-driven? No, we are supposed to be Holy Spirit driven. The one with the purpose is Jesus. You, my friend, have an assignment within that purpose.

What is Christ's purpose on the earth? First John 3:8 says, *"He who sins is of the devil, for the devil has sinned from the beginning. For this purpose the Son of God was manifested, that He might destroy the works of the devil."*

Your assignment in the army of God is your individual expression and extension of Christ's destruction of the works of the devil. You are a destroyer of the works of the devil. God will give you a way to do it that is all your own.

Until that gets through to you—until you admit and agree to those terms—God will remain silent about your assignment.

The word *purpose* is too general while an *assignment* is focused and deliberate. You can't image a professor saying, "Tonight's purpose is" when giving out homework. "Tonight's assignment" brings it right into focus.

Twice in the Old Testament we see prophets eaten by lions because they did not follow their direct instructions from God. Matthew Henry said, "Those whom God sends on his errands shall not go without full instructions."[1]

The purpose oriented can embellish God's order and add their own flavor and spin. Billy Graham was once offered tens of millions of dollars if he would build a college. He prayed and turned down the money because he knew it was not his assignment.[2]

Next, you must face the fact that very few are supposed to be preachers or pastors. For too long we have listened to the voice of God through a filter. Whenever God moved someone to serve, we assumed it meant ministry.

This assumption of ministry has sent many to Bible colleges who didn't belong there. Worse yet, it has filled pulpits with people who had no business being there. This reminds me of why President Woodrow Wilson once said, "One of the proofs of the divinity of our Gospel is the preaching it has survived."[3]

This filtered view of service is one big reason the Church lost influence in our nation. God tried to send people into education, law, medicine, business, art, media, and yes, even politics, but we herded them into "Christian service."

Jesus said, *"I do not pray that You should take them out of the world, but that You should keep them from the evil one"* (John 17:15). That means that we are the one religion in the world that does not need to hide or use violence. We are in the culture but not of the culture. We have the one faith that is designed to live behind enemy lines.

Esther and Daniel are timeless examples of pure vessels serving and influencing pagan cultures. Now prepare yourself for a greater shock: the secret to finding your assignment is your heart. God speaks to the heart and then the heart must control the mind. Today many Spirit-filled believers are practicing an unwitting form of New Age. They relate to God as if He were a force and not a person.

They think that audacity and confidence will unlock gifts, authority, and direction. They speak of "activating gifts" as if there was a formula to supernatural manifestations. My friend, it comes through brokenness, not arrogance. The "force" is a farce.

The Holy Spirit requires everything to come through relationship. Sorry, but Christianity has always been and will always be family owned and operated. So then how can we know our assignment?

The secret to your assignment is discovered in a strange and wonderful fact about God: He knows how to get the best out of His children. He gives them a love for something and then intensifies their passion. The key to your assignment is found in the love of your heart. God knows that if you are doing what you love, you will never give up. He knows you will endure whatever pain that is required. He knows you will sharpen your skills in an endeavor that is the love of your heart.

The way to test this is simple: when you think of your assignment, you do not immediately bask in the sense of glory about it; you instead take a true measure of the cost and the problems that this mission will cause—and it doesn't bother you.

Hannah wanted children. So then why did God close her womb? The Bible says He did. *"But to Hannah he would give a double portion, for he loved Hannah, although the Lord had closed her womb"* (1 Sam. 1:5). God was not being cruel; He was intensifying her desire for children.

To give up her firstborn to be a prophet required sacrifice. Love sacrifices. The kind of people who do harm to evil are capable of sacrifice. However, the current crop of those who shuttle in and out of "easy" church boast of all kinds of spirituality, but when things get real, they can't sacrifice.

By the way, Samuel was not God's total reward to Hannah. First Samuel 2:21 says, *"And the Lord visited Hannah, so that she conceived and bore three sons and two daughters. Meanwhile the child Samuel grew before the Lord."*

Find the love of your heart, and the money and skills will follow. So will instructions. Instructions come after love and not before. That is why First Corinthians 13 makes a great deal of the futility of service that is not out of love. Verse 3 says, *"And though I bestow all my goods to feed the poor, and though I give my body to be burned, but have not love, it profits me nothing."*

When I was a very young preacher, trying hard to know my assignment, David Wilkerson said this to me, "Mario, the will of God grows on you." How right he was.

From that moment on, Berkeley began to grow on me. I saw the riots on television, and the burden grew and grew for those students. Where did it grow? It grew in my heart. For you, it may be a passion to master a skill, it may be a people group you must help. You will find yourself more and more drawn to a specific field. No one but you and God may understand the reason for your choice. Even parents might have to let go of their original design for you. But out of the love of your heart.

But there is one final element to your assignment.

Because the American situation is impossible, only one kind of person will make a difference now. They must be armed with divine certainty. They must own an unshakable, to-the-bone conviction that they have been chosen for this task.

Without this, we have zero hope of removing the bloody talons of Satan off the throat of our nation. Without it, we are doomed to another embarrassing misfire pawned off as revival.

You see it in the Bible. You see it in the stories of heroes of faith throughout history who altered the course of their generation. At the dawn of their mission, God infuses them with incontestable certainty.

This certainty plays a critical role in their survival. Think of it like the escape velocity of a rocket. Escape velocity is one of the biggest challenges of space travel. In order for a rocket to break free of the earth's gravitational force, it must reach a speed of seven miles per second. That's 25,000 miles per hour!

Evil convulses at the approach of a new vessel of God. Hell instantly puts chosen ones on a hit list. The child of God must be blasted by divine certainty into a trajectory that will escape the pull of devils, the seduction of fame, withering criticism, and the dark night of the soul that comes to all who are called of God.

I will reuse a quote from an earlier chapter here. It is about William Wilberforce who was called by God in government to ban slavery. From his deathbed John Wesley wrote to encourage Wilberforce. In it he confirms the urgency of divine certainty: "Unless God has raised you up for this very thing, you will be worn out by the opposition of men and devils. But if God be for you, who can be against you? Are all of them together stronger than God? O be not weary of well doing! Go on, in the name of God and in the power of His might...."

Understand this, child of God! The same Spirit that is awakening a passion and direction in you is doing it to millions more. Soon an army will emerge that is entrenched in every area of our culture. Today it is fire here and there, but soon, as the prophetic core of God obey and embrace their assignment and come together in a chorus of victory, it will be unlike anything we have ever seen.

Chapter 13

THE PRICE OF GOD'S MIRACLE-WORKING POWER

You WANT TO SEE THE LAME WALK, THE BLIND SEE, AND the deaf hear? You want your days of powerless ministry to end? You want to unlock the how and why God grants power to do mighty signs and wonders? Do you wonder why so many have asked and so few have received the gift of healing and working of miracles?

It is time to peel back misconceptions. It is time to be brutally honest. We have been able to create mind-bending technological breakthroughs. We can now do in an instant what previously took decades, but we will never find a shortcut to supernatural power.

The Holy Spirit's work never changes. His process of taking raw material and making a living, breathing conduit of His power has never changed. In two thousand years, it has not been shortened or compromised one iota.

If you seek glamour and riches, skip this message. If you are dazzled by people you have seen powerfully used, save us both time, do not seek this power—you have no heart for it.

A young man—enthralled by the power he witnessed—ran up to Smith Wigglesworth and begged for the gift. Wigglesworth said, "You don't want it. Before God is through with you, you will feel as if a thousand switch trains have run over you." A. W. Tozer said, "It is doubtful whether God can bless a man greatly until He has hurt him deeply."[1]

You still yearn to be used? You still want power—real power and not the fluff of so many hyperemotional meetings today? Then proceed with caution.

The reason for our lack of power and miracles is plain. We are just not willing to pay the price. If you are willing, the Holy Spirit will take you through the process to power. Here then is the price of God's miracle-working power.

It All Begins with Self-Emptying

Listen to E. M. Bounds: "The preacher must throw himself, with all the abandon of a perfect, self-emptying faith and a self-consuming zeal, into his work for the salvation of men. Hearty, heroic, compassionate, fearless martyrs must the men be who take hold of and shape a generation for God."[2]

Again, A.W. Tozer said that these kinds of vessels "serve God and mankind from motives too high to be understood by the rank and file of religious retainers who today shuttle in and out of the sanctuary. They will make no decisions out of fear, take no course out of a desire to please, accept no service for financial considerations, perform no religious act out of mere custom; nor will they allow themselves to be influenced by the love of publicity or the desire for reputation."[3]

Oral Roberts despaired of life itself in his hunger to understand miracles. He was pastoring without power when he went to Kansas City to hear William Branham. That encounter with the supernatural was his line in the sand. He went into fasting and prayer. Oral went into the prayer closet and died.

In her desperation to understand the supernatural, Kathryn Kuhlman visited several healing meetings. She often left disgusted and brokenhearted. Her tears and prayers reached critical mass, and she made a holy vow to conduct meetings that were full of power and dignity.

She never looked back. Kathryn traced the moment of her power. She said, "I died." From that moment on, there was no Kathryn Kuhlman, only an utterly devoted shell.

COMPASSION

Oral Roberts, T. L. Osborn, Charles S. Price, and Aimee Semple McPherson all reported being overcome by compassion for the sick. Their level of caring rose to divine heights. They agonized for the lost, the sick, and the dying. Matthew 14:14 says, *"And when Jesus went out He saw a great multitude; and He was moved with compassion for them, and healed their sick."* Such compassion cannot be faked. It emanates from Christ Himself.

HATRED FOR SICKNESS AND EVIL

Few understand how the anointing is a product of hatred. Hebrews 1:9 says: *"You have loved righteousness and hated lawlessness; Therefore God, Your God, has anointed You with the oil of gladness more than Your companions."*

Alexander Dowie saw miracles after a plague struck his church in Sydney, Australia killing forty of his members. An inner rage transformed him until he called out to God with a pure heart and was rewarded with so much power that it left his entire congregation free of plague.

John G. Lake saw his wife die, and it unlocked a fury against evil that swept the world with healing.

POWER ALWAYS HAS A PURPOSE

And He was handed the book of the prophet Isaiah. And when He had opened the book, He found the place where it was written: "The Spirit of the Lord is upon Me, because He has anointed Me to preach the gospel to the poor; He has sent Me to heal the broken-hearted, to proclaim liberty to the captives and recovery of sight to the blind, to set at liberty those who are oppressed; to proclaim the acceptable year of the Lord" (Luke 4:17-19).

The most powerful part of those verses is this phrase: *"The Spirit of the Lord is upon Me, because."* Your "because" ruins you for all other plans, purposes, and goals. You must surrender to the one thing you are assigned to do. You must be able to list your purpose, articulate it simply and clearly, and execute it with extreme focus.

Every vessel of God has one life message. It is an outstanding theme of their life and a distillation of all that the Holy Spirit has ever had them say. T. L. Osborn's life reached millions and said something astonishing. His life said something that he never compromised or changed.

God is giving you power to do one special work. You cannot deviate from that divine intention. It will be a true work of God.

WAIT

Acts 1:4 says, *"And being assembled together with them, He commanded them not to depart from Jerusalem, but to wait for the Promise of the Father."* This is the key! Abraham could not wait. King Saul could not wait. Esau could not wait.

How long will you have to wait? *As long as it takes.* All the powers of hell will challenge your decision to wait. Satan has too much to lose if true healing power flows. It will not come easily. Your flesh will scream for release from your vigil.

Wait for true miracle power. Do not settle for the life you had before this quest. Your patience will be rewarded beyond measure. He will come in power. There will be no doubt.

This is the price of God's miracle-working power.

Chapter 14

BREAKING THE SPELL OF DEMONS OVER AMERICA

WHAT CAN WE DO ABOUT THE DEMONS THAT ARE strangling America? Can we break their spell over America? Divisive devils have brought us to the brink of civil war. Spirits of lust have spread the perversion that has contaminated every aspect of our culture. Demons have unleashed mass addiction and violence. Can we stop them?

Not only can we, it is our sworn duty to tear them down. The Bible says, *"For the weapons of our warfare are not carnal but mighty in God for pulling down strongholds, casting down arguments and every high thing that exalts itself against the knowledge of God"* (2 Cor. 10:4-5).

Most preaching and teaching today leaves the impression there is very little we can do. But that begs a question: If we can't tear down strongholds, isn't God guilty of child abuse on a grand scale? He is guilty of letting Paul awaken a deep hope that can never be fulfilled. The whole point of Second Corinthians 10:4-5 is to provoke the Church to take up the mighty weapons of God.

The Bible tells us in Luke 9:1, *"Then He called His twelve disciples together and gave them power and authority over all demons, and to cure diseases."* Matthew Henry comments on this verse: "He gave them authority over all devils, to dispossess them, and cast them out, though ever so numerous, so subtle, so fierce, so obstinate. Christ designed a total rout and ruin to the kingdom of darkness, and therefore gave them power over all devils."[1]

Lest we think this authority was somehow limited to the twelve, Mark 16:17 expounds: *"And these signs will follow those who believe: In My name they will cast out demons; they will speak with new tongues...."* The inference is overpowering. As many as can speak with tongues should also cast out devils.

But we need to see how Jesus looks from the demons' point of view. Let me give you an example of the utter helplessness of demons before Christ.

Matthew 8:28-29 says:

> *When He had come to the other side, to the country of the Gergesenes, there met Him two demon-possessed men, coming out of the tombs, exceedingly fierce, so that no one could pass that way. And suddenly they cried out, saying, "What have we to do with You, Jesus, You Son of God? Have You come here to torment us before the time?"*

When Jesus's foot touched the shore, it reverberated all the way up to the tomb. These men had thousands of devils. This horde of demons did not bother to run or hide from Christ. They ran down to Him and fell begging for mercy. His presence alone evokes pure terror in demons!

Why is there so little preached about actually taking ground back from the devil? There are many reasons. Satan has deceived the Church. But there are two deceptions that I believe make the Church passive.

These teachings must downplay victory over demons in order to stay in business. They are the therapeutic church and the gloom-and-doom church.

The therapeutic church must focus on happy talk and self-fulfillment. Shaking up their comfort zones with talk of warfare threatens attendance.

So many therapeutic preachers today love to say, "It's all in God's hands." While that is a comforting thought, it is misleading. God has chosen to act in response to prayer and faith. A lot of it is in our hands. That's why a key revival verse begins with *"If My people..."* (2 Chron. 7:14). This abuse of sovereignty—that God does it all on His own—has paralyzed Christians.

And even when we get around to espousing action, it is for selfish ends and toys not weapons. Those who teach only on wealth, success, and living the good life, are teaching a peacetime message in the middle of a war. They can't talk about how we are about to lose our nation. They tell you to have your best life now. But think about it, if this is your best life now, it means you are going to hell.

To survive, they must distract Christians to lesser goals and lower living. Measuring your spirituality by comfort ease and material pursuits cheapens the real purpose of the child of God. We are not supposed to bask by the pool; we are supposed to take cities. These motivational speakers are guilty of unwittingly helping the devil to keep the army of God distracted and powerless.

Then there's the gloom-and-doom church. Thegloom-and-doom message and the therapeutic message are opposite extremes; they both create a passive believer. The therapist preacher denies the existence of the war, and the gloom-and-doom preacher believes we must hunker down because we can't win.

The gloom and doomers keep the Church on the defensive because they believe victory is impossible. But let's be honest, fear sells books; conspiracy theories sell survival, not revival. Gloom-and-doom prophets secretly cheer on global domination, global warming, and global disasters to keep Christians buying stuff. They do not equip you for revival. They sell you equipment for survival.

They justify their dire instructions with Bible verses about the end times. But to properly understand end-time prophecy I must introduce you to the prophetic elephant.

But first, a folk tale from India about the elephant. It tells of six blind men approaching an elephant. The first blind man reached out and touched the side of the huge animal. "An elephant is smooth and solid like a wall!" he declared. "It must be very powerful."

The second blind man put his hand on the elephant's limber trunk. "An elephant is like a giant snake," he announced.

The third blind man felt the elephant's pointed tusk. "I was right," he decided. "This creature is as sharp and deadly as a spear."

The fourth blind man touched one of the elephant's four legs. "What we have here," he said, "is an extremely large cow."

The fifth blind man felt the elephant's giant ear. "I believe an elephant is like a huge fan or maybe a magic carpet that can fly over mountains and treetops," he said.

The sixth blind man gave a tug on the elephant's coarse tail. "Why, this is nothing more than a piece of old rope. Dangerous, indeed," he scoffed.

All these men were right, and they were all wrong. Likewise, if you were to lay end-time prophecy preachers end to end, they would point in all directions. This leaves the army with an uncertain sound for battle.

Now for the prophetic elephant. Those who teach that the end times are days of desperate evil and starvation are right. Those who predict a time of vast prosperity and breakthrough for the righteous are also right. It is correct to say that natural disasters await us, but it also correct to say that these will be times of refreshment, favor, and protection. It is true to say that we will go through some things, and it is equally true to say that we will escape many things. It is accurate to believe that men will be more perverted than ever, and on the other hand, that the glory of God will rise on the Church as never before. These are not contradictions, but rather prophetic paradoxes.

This paradox helps explain a world where the sublime and the vile advance together. This is the day of unlimited opportunity and unlimited disaster! How should we live in such a world? How do we make sense of prophecy? How do we best navigate these last days?

I believe that this paradox is meant to create an attitude in us. They force us to live in a dynamic tension. We must have respect for the dangers of our day and yet be bold to seize the open doors of the day. Someone once said, "Learn as if you will live forever and live as if you will die tomorrow."

The enemy uses all these imbalances to make the Church passive. But everywhere you look in the Bible it advocates action: *"Fight the good fight of faith"* (1 Tim. 6:12). *"Endure hardness as a good soldier"* (2 Tim. 2:3 KJV). *"Resist the devil"* (James 4:7). *"Take...the sword of the Spirit"* (Eph. 6:17).

God has chosen to act in answer to prayer. He waits until His people rise and take their rightful place in the arena of battle. Young David saw the stalemate. No one challenged Goliath. David couldn't stand it. He offered himself to God. We need someone like that today—someone who can't live with evil, who can't stomach the perversion, and is enraged to see God dishonored. Someone God can use to turn the tide of America.

All authority over devils is derived from the total victory of the cross. The next force to remember is the Blood of Jesus. The final force is the word of our testimony. These always and will always devastate both Satan and his imps. *"And they overcame him by the blood of the Lamb and by the word of their testimony, and they did not love their lives to the death"* (Rev. 12:11).

Total victory: What Jesus did to the devil on the cross was total victory. If only we could have been there when the crucified Christ kicked in the devil's teeth and stripped him of the keys of hell and the grave. Colossians 2:15 says, *"Having disarmed principalities and powers, He made a public spectacle of them, triumphing over them in it."*

There are many more things we can do to get out of fear and get into a great victory. Here is the great promise: when God sees someone take up the mighty weapons of God, in the name of Jesus, and attempt the impossible, God will muster all the resources of Heaven to bring that someone total victory.

Chapter 15

USHERING IN THE NEXT GREAT AWAKENING

REMEMBER I TOLD YOU THIS. IN THE NEXT FEW YEARS A new kind of Christian leader will appear. They will not fit any present mold. They will be the catalysts. They will usher in the next great awakening.

A few of them will be in pulpits. More of them will be in politics, business, science, law, entertainment, music, or a thousand other fields of endeavor. They will not introduce subjects; they will introduce eras.

No one will be able to buy them off or get them to change the subject. They will operate on a disquieting plane of holiness and consecration. I believe A. W. Tozer was describing them when he said, "They serve God and mankind from motives too high to be understood by the rank and file of religious retainers who today shuttle in and out of the sanctuary."

Today they suffer. Their agony is what happens when worlds collide. They see their destiny. It's big and dangerous. A part of them glories in the potential to know God intimately and represent

Him bravely. They see themselves rebuking kings, tyrants, and warmongers. They see themselves commanding the wealth of the wicked be handed over to the just.

They hear themselves speaking miracles over the hopeless and tormented. Golden ideas, purposes, tactics, and aspirations haunt them like angelic visitations.

They are a walking paradox. They feel weaker. They feel stronger. They feel disoriented. They feel focused. They feel discombobulated. They feel settled.

A side of them ponders the cost of greatness with fear and trembling. Another side of them exuberantly embraces the cost. They are reaching a tipping point in their misery. One of their worlds is about to be absorbed by the other.

Ushering in the next great awakening? Why not you? Surely you didn't get this far in this book by accident. You had many chances to put it down. You kept reading for a reason. You are going through the turmoil I just described. The Holy Spirit is ruining you to all other pursuits—you only seek to usher in the next great awakening. Am I right about you so far?

What you think of yourself does not matter. What He will do to and through you makes your age, education, talent, economic status, and popularity irrelevant.

The only thing that matters is what the Holy Spirit says. Max Lucado said, "God doesn't call the qualified, He qualifies the called. Don't let Satan convince you otherwise. Satan will tell you that God has an IQ requirement or an entry fee... that he employs only specialists and experts, governments and high-powered personalities."[1]

There is only one way for you to find relief. You must surrender to the holy work of God. Paul put it this way, *"That I may lay hold of that for which Christ Jesus has also laid hold of me"* (Phil. 3:12). How else can I say this? Get hold of what has gotten hold of you. Grab on to what is grabbing you.

Of course, you are grappling with the cost. Of course, you are in deep turmoil living between worlds. But there is a tipping point when you will give in. What is that point?

When the pain of being average becomes stronger than the fear of greatness, you will embrace your destiny. You hurt so bad, facts will no longer count. Your lack of talent, training, age, or any future suffering cease to matter.

The Holy Spirit is separating you unto Him for a work He has for you. You feel that separation not just from people but from regular ideas. You feel that none of the changes you are going through fit any current career. You are right. The world you fit into has not yet arrived. The outpouring of God that will reveal the context of your gift isn't here yet.

The faith He is forging in you—the biases and prejudices He is extracting from you, the agony and ecstasy that tempers you—is not for what is happening now but for what will happen next.

The great danger I face is to over-teach you on how to prepare to usher in the next great awakening. That is because your assignment is exotic and unprecedented. Because there has never been anyone like you, I must be careful what I tell you.

The mentors in the Bible faced this challenge. Eli the priest had never seen a Samuel before. Samuel in turn had never seen a David before. Certainly, the church in Jerusalem did not know what to make of Saul of Tarsus. If they had tried to conform these new breeds into old models, they could have doused an original flame God was introducing to the world.

However, there are universal truths in the Bible that must live in every vessel of God. Those who usher in awakenings carry classic traits. They are listed in these verses:

> *But in a great house there are not only vessels of gold and silver, but also of wood and clay, some for honor and some for dishonor. Therefore if anyone cleanses himself from the latter, he will be a vessel for honor, sanctified and useful for the Master, prepared for every good work.* (2 Timothy 2:20-21).

THEY ARE CLEANSED FROM THE ELEMENTS OF WOOD AND CLAY

This is talking about people—people you need to get clear of. They contaminate your faith and lower your purity and urgency. Your inner circle of friends must not only share your passion, they must also be able to provoke you to good works.

God is going to tell you some amazing things—things you can't say around just anyone. The wrong people will fill you with unbelief. The wrong people will lower your moral standards, especially your sense of urgency.

THEY ARE VESSELS UNTO HONOR

The golden vessels in the temple served a sacred purpose. They were created for that purpose and were treasured for that purpose. That same quality permeates all who are used of the Holy Spirit for greatness. The only difference is that the people God chooses feel profoundly honored to be chosen.

Let me explain what that sense of honor is. These vessels have been invited to be used of God. They are honored to have been chosen. That honor breaks them. It overwhelms them. They have no words to express how they feel that God has so honored them as to be part of His work.

You will remember the disciples in Acts 5:41: *"So they departed from the presence of the council, rejoicing that they were counted worthy to suffer shame for His name."* If that is how they felt about the privilege of being beaten, how do you think they valued prayer, preaching, and personal discipline. Their deepest sorrow would come from displeasing the Lord who had honored them by calling them. No wonder Paul called it a high calling.

How unlike the crop of leaders who feel entitled? Those who ooze with an air of casual faith and feel they are doing God a favor by serving Him.

A vessel unto honor carries soberness of heart about their mission. Their souls sit with Christ in heavenly places. They carry an awareness of the realm of the spirit that is more real to them than the natural world.

Evan Roberts seemed strange. Even those closest to him could not always understand why he acted the way he acted. In his early twenties he began to be aware that something was coming—that God's dealings were leading up to something. Sometimes that awareness gave him a blank stare and he could remain motionless for hours.

Often his friends would see him standing by the side of the road staring and as still as a statue. In church he had the ability to listen so intently it actually scared people. What was wrong with this man? He was being fitted for a Godsend. He revered the preparation.

But his seriousness of purpose also manifested itself in uncontrollable sobbing in extended prayer and vast absorption of the Bible. He knew he was being fitted for war. Nothing could come between him and his assignment.

God told Roberts that a massive awakening was coming to Wales and one hundred thousand men would be converted. In fact, Roberts openly confessed it. He also believed that when the awakening hit, those one hundred thousand men would be saved within five years. He was mistaken. It happened in two years.

THEY ARE SANCTIFIED AND USEFUL FOR THE MASTER

How does God cleanse a man or a woman for service? He makes you desperate. How does He make you desperate? He knows how to make you want things. He knows how to deepen passion.

But before we get to that let's consider why a clean vessel is so useful. A pure heart can be trusted. When God imparts gifts, talents, power, and authority to someone, that someone is going to make some noise. Crowds will form. Money will appear.

All that can conspire to destroy the unforged vessel. A compromised servant is useless. Desperation is a holy soap. I will repeat something I said before about Hannah.

We face a new kind of evil. We have never faced a threat like this before. That is why God is creating special kinds of people to be used in special kinds of ways. What do these people look like?

We picture bold, assertive, natural-born leaders taking the stage. We assume the Holy Spirit would instill great confidence and audacity in those He has selected for special service.

In fact, the opposite is true. He inflicts those He chooses with deep frustrations. They are restless; they are weakened by confusing emotions. Often they don't feel very spiritual at all. The greatest gift He gives them is a desperate hunger.

In fact, your deep frustrations are a sign that God is going to use you mightily because they create desperate hunger.

Yes, desperate hunger is a great gift. Although, when you first get it, you will be convinced you are being punished not blessed.

Jesus said, *"Blessed are those who hunger and thirst..."* (Matt. 5:6). It seems a contradictory statement, but a closer look reveals eternal wisdom.

God is carving out your soul to create a greater capacity for His power. You are getting desperate for something—your appetite for that one thing is increasing. It seems cruel, but it makes perfect sense. God wants you to want something you can't have. It is in the not having it that your desire intensifies.

The Bible says, *"But to Hannah he would give a double portion, for he loved Hannah, although the Lord had closed her womb. And her rival also provoked her severely, to make her miserable, because the Lord had closed her womb"* (1 Sam. 1:5-6).

Look at that! God is creating unbearable frustration. But by depriving her of children, it increased two things in her soul: her willingness to sacrifice and her appreciation for the blessings when they came. In other words, she is an amazing example of willingness and appreciation.

God didn't want Hannah to get over wanting children. He wanted her to yearn for them even more. The end result is one of the most powerful women in history—the mother of Samuel the prophet. In Jewish tradition Samuel is second only to Moses as a prophet.

Hannah's total reward often goes unnoticed. True, she surrendered her firstborn to God, but it says in First Samuel 2:21, *"And the Lord visited Hannah, so that she conceived and bore three sons and two daughters. Meanwhile the child Samuel grew before the Lord."*

I saw one of the most acute cases of deep yearning in my life in a small town in the mountains of California. I am talking a small town—I think the phone book had one yellow page. (I wrote that so many who do not know what a yellow page is will have to look it up.) Anyway...

This young pastor's father asked me if I would go preach for his son. Each time I went, the young man who led the church got worse and worse. By that I mean he got desperate.

One night something happened so intense, that all these years later it feels like it just happened. After the service we sat and talked. I looked at him, and he began to weep. He yearned to see signs and wonders. It was the most desperate cry I had ever seen. His passion to see Jesus heal seemed like it was about to kill him.

But I knew he was on the verge of a Godsend. I knew he would see exceeding, abundantly more than he could ask or think. I knew that his insatiable heart's cry was cleansing him for an astounding work. The dad was Earl Johnson. You know his son, Bill Johnson.

Unbearable hunger for an awakening can be painful. You will yearn for a sign that your hunger will be fulfilled. You will yearn for proof that you will not die from disappointment. Well beloved, the proof is right under your nose. The hunger itself is the proof of the fulfillment.

Jesus said, *"Blessed are those who hunger and thirst for righteousness, for they shall be filled"* (Matt. 5:6). In other words, if you hunger, you are blessed because that is the proof you shall be filled.

Alexander MacLaren, the great Bible commentator, said, "That hunger is the sure precursor and infallible prophet of the coming satisfaction."[2]

PREPARED FOR EVERY GOOD WORK

A breed of Christian is coming to turn America away from destruction. We are running out of time. They will be bold, creative, compelling, and express the deep love of God like a light in the darkness. But there is one more thing they will be, and no one predicted it better than Smith Wigglesworth.

On August 11, 1929, Smith Wigglesworth preached at Angelus Temple in Los Angeles. He had issued a solemn warning about the last days and how half the Body of Christ would not be ready. Then he said there was something we must all do:

> Up to this present time the Lord's word is for us: "Hitherto ye have asked nothing." (See John 16:24.) Surely you people that have been asking great things from God for a long time would be amazed, if you entered into it with clear knowledge that it is the Master, it is Jesus, who has such knowledge of the mightiness of the power of the Father and of the joint union with Him that nothing is impossible for you to

ask. Surely it is He only who could say "Hitherto you have asked nothing."

So God means me to press you another step forward. Begin to believe on extravagant asking, believing that God is pleased when you ask large things." [3]

We have entered a time of extravagant asking. It is time to ask God for the impossible and the unimaginable. These askers are coming. It is that element in the vessel of God that is prepared for every good work. These are greater works that Jesus declared when He said, *"Most assuredly, I say to you, he who believes in Me, the works that I do he will do also; and greater works than these he will do, because I go to My Father"* (John 14:12).

It's no violation of the Scripture to believe the last days still hold an unseen intervention. The proof a Godsend is possible is so simple, it is easy to miss. The proof is the fact that we are still here. Second Corinthians 2:14 says, *"Now thanks be to God who always leads us in triumph in Christ, and through us diffuses the fragrance of His knowledge in every place."* The first duty of any general is to take his soldiers out of certain annihilation.

The next proof is the widespread dealing of the Holy Spirit. He is stirring millions to action. He is not instructing us on an exit strategy but a confrontation with evil.

A further proof of the intense passion of God to save America: our history is a record of intervention just before our destruction that has been repeated again and again. Who are you and I to say it can't happen? I assure you that Satan is in for the fight of his life to take down America.

But I leave you with a final challenge. What if the best churches haven't even been planted yet? What if the greatest sermons are yet to be preached? What if the best inventions, books, songs, and miracles are yet to come? I wouldn't doubt it. God always saves the best for last.

NOTES

INTRODUCTION THE GODSEND

1. A. W. Tozer, *Tozer Speaks, Volume One* (Camp Hill, PA: WingSpread Publishers, 1994).
2. Dennis Prager, "The Left Will Make 2019 a Dark Year," DennisPrager .com & Salem National, January 3, 2019, https://www.dennisprager .com/the-left-will-make-2019-a-dark-year/.

CHAPTER 1 BEFORE THERE CAN BE A GREAT AWAKENING, THERE MUST BE A RUDE AWAKENING

1. Abraham Lincoln, *The Portable Abraham Lincoln,* ed. Andrew Delbanco (New York: Penguin Books, 2009).

CHAPTER 2 WHY SATAN MUST DESTROY AMERICA

1. Ludwig von Mises, *Theory and History* (Auburn, AL: Ludwig von Mises Institute, 1985), 51.
2. Joel C. Rosenberg, "Islamic Extremists Are Trying to Hasten the Coming of the Mahdi," National Review, September 11, 2015, https://www.nationalreview.com/2015/09/radical-islam-iran-isis -apocalytpic-messiah-mahdi/.
3. Von Mises, *Theory and History,* 51.
4. George Orwell, *The Collected Essays, Journalism, and Letters of George Orwell*, ed. Sonia Orwell and Ian Angus (Boston: David R. Godine Publisher, 2000), 137.

CHAPTER 4 WHY THE TIME IS NOW

1. Edward M. Bounds, *Power Through Prayer* (Shippensburg, PA: Destiny Image, 2007).
2. "Is God Dead?", *Time*, April 8, 1966.
3. Thomas J. Moore and Donald R. Mattison, "Adult Utilization of Psychiatric Drugs and Differences by Sex, Age, and Race," *Journal*

of the American Medical Association Internal Medicine 177, no. 2 (2017): 274-275.

4. Rhitu Chatterjee, "Americans Are a Lonely Lot, and Young People Bear the Heaviest Burden," NPR, May 1, 2018, https://www.npr.org/sections/health-shots/2018/05/01/606588504/americans-are-a-lonely-lot-and-young-people-bear-the-heaviest-burden.

5. Najja Parker, "Study: The More Social Media You Use, the Lonelier You Feel," *Atlanta Journal Constitution*, March 7, 2017, https://www.ajc.com/news/study-the-more-social-media-you-use-the-lonelier-you-feel/BMrMDGi4ylrt3I569YZvNO/.

6. Grace Donnelly, "Here's Why Life Expectancy in the U.S. Dropped Again This Year," Fortune Media IP Limited, February 9, 2018, http://fortune.com/2018/02/09/us-life-expectancy-dropped-again/.

CHAPTER 5 THE CRIME OF CHURCH GROWTH WITHOUT THE HOLY SPIRIT

1. Scot McKnight, "Growing Pains: The Purpose-Driven Church Model," Patheos, September 11, 2006, https://www.patheos.com/blogs/jesuscreed/2006/09/11/growing-pains-the-purpose-driven-church-model/.

2. Charles Finney, *Experiencing the Presence of God* (New Kensington, PA: Whitaker House, 2000).

3. Michael Snyder, "The Dying Church—100 Churches Will Close This Week," Prophecy News Watch, November 30, 2018, http://prophecynewswatch.com/article.cfm?recent_news_id=2778.

4. Matthew Henry, *Matthew Henry's Commentary on the Whole Bible: Volume IV–IV—Joel to Malachi,* ed. Anthony Uyl (Ontario: Devoted Publishing, 2017), 37.

CHAPTER 6 THE CRIME OF NOT JUDGING RIGHTEOUSLY

1. Charles Dickens, *A Christmas Carol* (London: William Heinemann, 1906), 70, 82–85.

2. Paul Copan and William Lane Craig, eds., *Passionate Convictions* (Nashville: B&H Publishing Group, 2007), 12.

CHAPTER 7 THE CRIME OF FALSE SUBMISSION TO GOVERNMENT

1. Charles G. Finney, *Lectures on Systematic Theology,* ed. Richard Friedrich (Fairfax, VA: Xulon Press, 2002), 480.
2. Charles Finney, *Power from on High* (Fort Washington, PA: CLC Publications, 2005).
3. John Wesley, *John Wesley: An Autobiographical Sketch of the Man and His Thought, Chiefly from His Letters,* ed. Ole E. Borgen (Leiden, Netherlands: E. J. Brill, 1966), 110.
4. Eric Metaxas, *Bonhoeffer Study Guide: The Life and Writings of Dietrich Bonhoeffer* (Nashville: Thomas Nelson, 2014), 59.

CHAPTER 8 THE CRIME OF ABUSING GRACE AND HOLINESS

1. "Amazing Grace" by John Newton, 1779, public domain.
2. Dietrich Bonhoeffer, *The Cost of Discipleship* (New York: Touchstone, 1995), 43.
3. Bonhoeffer, *The Cost of Discipleship*, 44–45.

CHAPTER 9 THE CRIME OF THE CONTAMINATED CROWD

1. Evan Andrews, "What Killed Harry Houdini?", A&E Television Networks, LLC, updated August 22, 2018, https://www.history.com/news/what-killed-harry-houdini.
2. *Blue Letter Bible,* s.v. "*planáō,*" accessed May 2, 2019, https://www.blueletterbible.org/lang/lexicon/lexicon.cfm?Strongs=G4105&t=KJV.
3. Bible Hub, s.v. "*planaō,*" accessed May 2, 2019, https://biblehub.com/greek/4105.htm.
4. Matthew Henry, *An Exposition of the Old and New Testament,* vol. 4 (New York: Robert Carter and Brothers, 1856), 115.

Chapter 10 The Crime of Withholding the Baptism in the Holy Spirit

1. C. H. Spurgeon, *The Soul Winner* (Dallas: Gideon House Books, 2016).

Chapter 11 Separate to Me

1. David Wilkerson, "End-Time Values," World Challenge Pulpit Series, last updated March 26, 2006, http://www.tscpulpitseries.org/english/undated/tsendtim.html.
2. Smith Wigglesworth, *Smith Wigglesworth on Heaven* (New Kensington, PA: Whitaker House, 1998).

Chapter 12 Your Assignment in the Godsend

1. Matthew Henry, *Matthew Henry's Commentary on the Whole Bible: Volume II-I: First Kings to Esther,* ed. Anthony Uyl (Ontario: Devoted Publishing, 2017), 164.
2. Harold Myra and Marshall Shelley, *The Leadership Secrets of Billy Graham* (Grand Rapids, MI: Zondervan, 2010).
3. Paul Jersild, *Invitation to Faith* (Eugene, OR: Wipf and Stock Publishers, 2018).

Chapter 13 The Price of God's Miracle-Working Power

1. A. W. Tozer, *The Root of Righteousness* (Chicago: Moody Publishers, 2015).
2. E. M. Bounds, *The Works of E. M. Bounds* (Zeeland, MI: Reformed Church Publications, 2009), 3.
3. A. W. Tozer, *Of God and Men* (Chicago: Moody Publishers, 2015).

Chapter 14 Breaking the Spell of Demons Over America

1. Matthew Henry, *Matthew Henry's Commentary on the Whole Bible: Volume V-II: Mark–Luke*, ed. Anthony Uyl (Ontario: Devoted Publishing, 2018), 207.

Chapter 15 Ushering in the Next Great Awakening

1. Max Lucado, "Qualifying the Called," accessed May 3, 2019, https://maxlucado.com/listen/qualifying-the-called/.
2. Alexander MacLaren, *MacLaren's Commentary* (Harrington, DE: Delmarva Publications, 2013).
3. Smith Wigglesworth, *Smith Wigglesworth on Power Scripture* (New Kensington, PA: Whitaker House, 2009).

ABOUT
MARIO MURILLO

Mario Murillo rose from poverty in the Mission District of San Francisco. After being revolutionized by Christ, he felt a call to the riot-torn University of California at Berkeley. He was rejected until a desperate prayer season resulted in supernatural power. It began with preaching different than any the students had ever heard. Then the students began to report healings in the Name of Jesus. A four-day crusade in San Jose, California, lasting six months with a total of over 250,000 people, birthed an international ministry that is reaching millions!

Made in the USA
Middletown, DE
28 October 2020

20781576R00089